Political Traditions in Foreign Policy Series

KENNETH W. THOMPSON, Editor

*Foreign Policy
in the Early Republic*

Foreign Policy
in the Early Republic

THE LAW OF NATIONS
AND THE BALANCE OF POWER

Daniel George Lang

Louisiana State University Press
Baton Rouge and London

Designer: Christopher Wilcox
Typeface: Galliard
Typesetter: G & S Typesetters
Printer: Thomson-Shore, Inc.
Binder: John Dekker & Sons, Inc.

Library of Congress Cataloging in Publication Data

Lang, Daniel George.
    Foreign policy in the early republic.
    (Political traditions in foreign policy series)
    Bibliography: p.
    Includes index.
    1. United States—Foreign relations—1783–1815.
2. International law.   3. Balance of power.   I. Title.
II. Series.
JX1412.L36 1985   341.5   85-11341
ISBN 0-8071-1255-0

Contents

Acknowledgments

"A teacher affects eternity," wrote Henry Adams; "he can never tell where his influence stops." Teaching in this case includes models worth emulating as well as substantive ideas and approaches, and I have been influenced in both ways by my teachers. Kenneth W. Thompson has provided constant encouragement, wise counsel, and insightful criticism. He has sustained me in more ways than he knows. Inis L. Claude, Jr., made countless suggestions which greatly improved the quality of this work, and Norman Graebner gave helpful advice and support in the final stages of writing. I am deeply grateful to each of these teachers for their contributions to this study.

The White Burkett Miller Center of Public Affairs and the H. B. Earhart Foundation provided generous financial support which made it possible to complete my work. I would only hope that I can partially repay these debts by striving to achieve the excellence in teaching and writing to which these institutions and individuals are committed.

Beverly Jarrett, Catherine Barton, and Marie Blanchard of LSU Press provided all the editorial support and guidance one could hope for.

Finally, Heidi, my wife, who does not regard herself as a teacher, nevertheless exerted the greatest influence; without her unfailing encouragement, steadfast love, and constant support this endeavor would not have been possible.

Foreign Policy
in the Early Republic

The Just War, the Law of Nations, and the Balance of Power

Just-war theorists and balance of power theorists often seem to talk past each other in discussions about war and international relations. This divergence seems explicable on the basis of language alone: just-war theories are formulated in Latin, balance of power theories in German or French. The former concern themselves with morality and the law of nations, the latter with military strategy, geopolitics, and the national interest. The former come from the reflections of moralists, theologians, and political theorists, the latter from diplomats, stategists, and statesmen. Sometimes adherents of one approach may abuse those of the other: just-war champions reducing balance of power advocates to mere power politicians, and balance of power thinkers condemning just-war theorists as crusaders or as virtual pacifists. For the most part, however, advocates of both approaches may be regarded as members of a common, if not always harmonious, moral and intellectual household. When President Washington in his Proclamation of Neutrality declared that "the duty and interest of the United States require, that they should with sincerity and good faith adopt and pursue a conduct friendly and impartial towards the belligerent Powers,"[1] he asserted an identity of morality and policy which had been and would be repeated time and again. This, I suggest, was not an aberration, but was consistent with the received

1. Cited in Harold Syrett and Jacob Cooke (eds.), *The Papers of Alexander Hamilton* (26 vols.; New York, 1961–79), XIV, 308–309, n. 2.

1

opinion of the science of international law and politics of that day, for which the question of the just war was a primary moral and political concern. Before discussing that science and the evidence for its influence on the founding fathers, one must understand something of its origins.

The science of international law and politics which emerged with modern political thought can be seen in part as a response to the century of religion-inspired international and civil wars which accompanied the Reformation and subsequent Hapsburg efforts to restore the Catholic unity of Europe. The immense destruction and deep sense of insecurity those wars produced provoked concerned men to consider how war might be restrained and limited, if not eliminated. This required a reappraisal of ancient and medieval thought and led to the establishment of the new science.

The medieval doctrine of the just war, one idea which underwent reexamination, had roots in ancient theory and practice. Cicero took note of the Roman ceremonial of the Fetial College, a ritual conducted by a religious body prior to the initiation of hostilities and without which the war would be judged unjust and unholy. The Romans, then, tied the problem of the just war closely with the question of right authority; they concerned themselves less with the just and unjust reasons for the resort to force or with what constitutes just conduct in war. Classical political philosophy in general, while it mentioned just and unjust wars, never made a real effort to elaborate a full-fledged just-war theory; external matters were most often left to the discretion of wise and prudent rulers. Such matters could not be legislated because they depended on ever-changing and usually unforeseeable circumstances; of more importance was the cultivation of moral and intellectual qualities which would enable rulers to rule well.[2]

For the church fathers the problem of warfare had much more urgency, given the force of the biblical teaching concerning the sacredness of life. Could a Christian, i.e., someone animated by the

2. Cicero, *On the Commonwealth*, trans. G. H. Sabine and Stanley B. Smith (New York, 1929), 166–73; Ernest L. Fortin, "Christianity and the Just-War Theory," *Orbis* (Fall, 1983), 525–26.

precepts of Christian love, ever justifiably participate in war? Starting with Augustine, the theologians and canonists answered: Yes, but only under certain specified conditions or criteria; otherwise the moral prohibition against killing takes precedence. Over time these criteria became more refined and included the following: right authority, just cause, right intention, reasonable hope of success, proportionality, last resort, end of peace, and just conduct. The intention of all this, as James T. Johnson has emphasized, was to sanction and limit war simultaneously.[3]

This tradition, however, had given rise to a holy war or crusade analogue in which a religious authority sanctioned the resort to force for some explicitly religious reason. The original crusades were authorized by the popes to regain Jerusalem and to save the Christian holy places from the infidel Turks. Later, in the Counter-Reformation, Catholics were asked to defend the faith against the onslaught of the heretical Protestants, who in turn availed themselves of religious appeals in calling down the wrath of heaven against the "Whore of Babylon," the papacy. Critics of these wars believed that such appeals only encouraged hatred and contributed greatly to the savagery of the wars. It seemed especially ironic that Christianity, ostensibly the religion of love, could inspire such ruthlessness. Whereas religious war did not necessarily lead to indiscriminate violence—Johnson remarks on the discipline and restraint of Cromwell's armies—it seemed logical to critics that a person who assumed that he was acting as God's agent would have few scruples about what he did under that aegis. In such cases the elementary rules of political psychology would overrule the rigors of moral and theological constructs.[4]

One solution to the problem of religious war was to declare all

3. James T. Johnson, *Just War Tradition and the Restraint of War* (Princeton, 1981), xxix; James F. Childress, "Just-War Theories," *Theological Studies* XXXIX (1978), 427–45. Other works on this subject are E. B. F. Midgeley, *The Natural Law Tradition and the Theory of International Relations* (London, 1975), William O'Brien, *The Conduct of Just and Limited War* (New York, 1981), Frederick Russell, *The Just War in the Middle Ages* (Cambridge, England, 1975), and Michael Walzer, *Just and Unjust Wars* (New York, 1977).
4. Leroy Walters, "The Just War and the Crusade: Antitheses or Analogies?" *Monist*, LVII (October, 1973), 584–94; Russell, *The Just War in the Middle Ages*, 250–89.

wars irrational and immoral. The great Christian humanist Erasmus took this position, making him, according to Michael Howard, the first in a long line of humanitarian thinkers for whom it was enough to chronicle the horrors of war in order to condemn it. For Erasmus, "there is nothing more wicked, more disastrous, more widely destructive, more deeply tenacious, more loathsome, in a word, more unworthy of man, not to say a Christian," than war.[5]

The other, more common, position was that war as such was not always irrational or immoral, but that religious wars were. It was out of this view that the modern law of nations emerged. Gentili, Vitoria, Grotius, Locke, and Vattel all rejected religious motives as a just cause for war, although they asserted the possibility of just war on other grounds.[6] Francis Bacon went so far as to say that sanctions against wars for religion ought to be incorporated into religious teaching itself: "Therefore it is most necessary that the church by doctrine and decree, princes by their sword, and all learnings, both Christian and moral, do damn and send to hell for ever those facts and opinions tending to the support of [war for religion]."[7]

Thus the emphasis in just-war thinking shifted from the theological to secular foundations, or to put it another way, from a charity-based morality to one of natural rights. As a result, the authority of the pope faded and the medieval just-war criteria were redefined,

---

5. Michael Howard, *War and the Liberal Conscience* (New Brunswick, N.J., 1978), 15–16.

6. For Gentili's rejection of the resort to force for the sake of religion see the translated excerpts of his *De Jure Belli* in M. Forsyth, H. Keens-Soper, and P. Savigear (eds.), *The Theory of International Relations* (London, 1970), 15–35. On Vitoria see the comments of Alberto Coll, *Law, Theology, and History* (Washington, D.C., 1982), 22–23, and Johnson, *Just War Tradition*, 94–103. For the views of Grotius see the "Prolegomena," of *The Law of War and Peace*, sec. 11; Locke implies the same view in *The Second Treatise of Government*, Chaps. 2 and 3. Grotius condemns wars motivated by the desire to spread the gospel by force in *The Law of War and Peace*, Book II, Chap. 22, as does Vattel in *The Law of Nations*, Book III, Chap. 3. Quincy Wright prefers a positivist conception of international law for similar reasons in Quincy Wright, "International Law and Ideologies," *American Journal of International Law*, XLVIII (October, 1954), 615–30.

7. Francis Bacon, "Of Unity in Religion," *Essays* (London, 1972), 11–12.

4

modified, or dropped. Where the pope once claimed the authority to allocate the newly discovered lands in the Far East and in the Western Hemisphere as head of the church, first possession and the freedom of the seas became the natural-rights bases for the disposition of new discoveries.[8] The sovereign or prince was given the final word in the resort to war with the church's voice clearly subordinate; the right of self-defense replaced the punishment of wrongdoing or the protection of the innocent as just cause for war (thereby preparing the way for the development of the rights of neutrality); right intention disappeared as external actions assumed much greater importance; the just/unjust dichotomy gave way to an assumption of "simultaneous ostensible justice"; and emphasis shifted from limiting entry into war (*jus ad bellum*) to limiting a state's conduct in war (*jus in bello*). In short, the desire to manage war and moderate conflict which had been part of the just-war tradition remained, but the experience of religious warfare made writers of the law of nations anxious to delegitimize religion-based grounds for the resort to force.[9]

The second medieval ideal which came under attack concerned the desirability of "universal monarchy" or world empire. This question raised the issue of justice in another way: what kind and scale of government would best secure for men their due and their happiness? Classical political theory regarded empire with distaste. It taught that justice was possible only in small face-to-face communities devoted to the cultivation of a certain way of life. Plato's account of justice began with the treatment of it as a quality which exists in a whole community and was predicated on a quality of friendship which binds that community together. Empires are simply too big to permit this, and they also encourage the cultivation of less desirable characteristics among their citizens. This view was echoed in Augus-

8. James T. Johnson, *Ideology, Reason, and the Limitation of War* (Princeton, 1975), 157; Adolph Rein, "Über die Bedeutung der Überseeischen Ausdehnung für das europaische Stattensystem," *Historische Zeitschrift*, CXXXVII (1927), 28–90.
9. Johnson, *Ideology, Reason, and the Limitation of War*, Chaps. 3 and 4; Gentili in Forsyth *et al.* (eds.), *The Theory of International Relations*, 25–29; Joachim von Elbe, "The Evolution of the Concept of the Just War in International Law," *American Journal of International Law*, XXX (October, 1939), 665–88.

tine, who compared the scale of government with the size of the human body to suggest that great size is not necessarily desirable: "Why must a kingdom be distracted in order to be great? In this little world of man's body is it not better to have a moderate stature, and health with it, than to attain the huge dimensions of a giant by unnatural torments, and when you attain it find no rest, but to be pained the more in proportion to the size of your members?"[10] This tradition, which was not optimistic about the possibility of achieving justice, suggested that the interests of humanity are best served within small, highly regulated communities largely isolated from one another. Statesmanlike prudence here stressed moderation and concern with community character and integrity. That statesmen were authorized to protect the innocent and punish wrongdoing provided a check on the size and ambitions of other states, though classical political thought stressed "the primacy of internal policy."[11]

Medieval Christendom drew much more heavily on the example of the unity of Europe under Roman law than on the Greek *polis* which had been the inspiration of classical thought. Guided by the majesterial role of the Roman Catholic Church, it sought to establish cultural unity among much larger populations than the ancients would have thought desirable. The emphasis here is on world order and unity of rule, which make possible the greatest of goods necessary to human happiness, that is, universal peace. For Dante, the most forceful exponent of this view, it followed that "since it appears that the whole of mankind is ordained to one end, as we proved above, it should therefore have a single rule and government, and this power should be called the Monarch or Emperor. And thus it is plain for the well-being of the world, there must be a single world-rule or empire."[12] When Charles V, the Holy Roman Emperor, undertook to reunite Europe in the name of Catholicism, he was fighting as well to

10. Augustine, *The City of God*, trans. Marcus Dods (New York, 1950), Book III, Chap. 10; for a similar analogy see Grotius, *The Law of War and Peace*, Book II, Chap. 22.
11. Leo Strauss, *The Political Philosophy of Hobbes* (Chicago, 1952), 161; Fortin, "Christianity and the Just-War Theory," 525.
12. Dante, *On World Government*, trans. Herbert Schneider (Indianapolis, 1957), Book 1, Chap. 12.

sustain this great good of universal monarchy.[13] In the seventeenth century Louis XIV would be charged with seeking this same goal. French envy would soon make the same accusation against the efforts of Great Britain to attain universal empire at sea. These accusations and counter-accusations spilled across the Atlantic onto American shores in the 1790s: Federalists interpreted French declarations as tending to universal empire, while democratic-republicans dwelled on Britain's mastery of the seas and control of overseas trade as the main threat.[14]

Critics in the sixteenth, seventeenth, and eighteenth centuries saw in "universal monarchy" a formula for world tyranny, but found in the emerging balance of power system the key to prevent it. Such a system required only that several states persist as independent loci of power, capable of checking the ambitions of others. Wars would still be a feature of human relations, but they would be limited in aims and in means. First, statesmen would realize that attempts to overturn the system would probably fail because of the opposition of other states. This would encourage them to seek essentially marginal advantages rather than outright control of other states. Here the just-war criterion "hope of success" assumed a more prominent role than in the classic formulation where it was overshadowed by considerations of just causes. Herbert Butterfield notes that "it is far easier to control a war when your aim is the occupation of a particular territory or city, than when your aim is the eradication of militarism or making the world safe for democracy." Restraint in victory rather than unconditional surrender was another important consequence of the limited balance of power system; today's enemy may well be needed as tomorrow's ally and today's ally may well become tomorrow's adversary.[15]

13. Charles Davenant, *Essays Upon the Balance of Power, the Right of Making War, Peace, and Alliances, and Universal Monarchy* (London, 1701), 277–83; Alexander Hamilton, John Jay, and James Madison, *The Federalist Papers* (New York, 1961), 55.
14. Gerald Stourzh, *Alexander Hamilton and the Idea of Republican Government* (Stanford, 1970), 140; Rein, "Über die Bedeutung der Überseeischen Ausdehnung," 61–73.
15. Robert Osgood, *Limited War Revisited* (Boulder, Colorado, 1979), 3; Butterfield is cited in Coll, *Law, Theology, and History*, 75. Unlike the international jurists

Second, to focus on marginal advantages was to focus on mundane, limited objectives such as security, wealth, or territory. It would make little sense for an army seeking to take a rich province to devastate that province and destroy what made it desirable in the first place. Power and wealth reinforced each other, but they were limiting factors as well, particularly for monarchs who had to finance their wars themselves. The difficulty and expense of raising, equipping, and maintaining professional armies of the seventeenth and eighteenth centuries made monarchs and generals reluctant to engage in battle, preferring to conduct campaigns of sieges. To compel an adversary to make peace because of one's superior strategic position or his financial exhaustion seemed preferable to staking all in a battle in which advantages accrued over several years might be thrown away in as many hours, "especially," remarks Howard, "since the political objectives for which the wars were fought were seldom such as to justify such bloody solutions."[16] These limitations made sovereigns acutely aware of the need to weigh the costs and the benefits of engaging in war; or in just-war language, the evil produced by the war must not be greater than the good done or the evil averted by it. This involved a moral as well as a political, economic, or military accounting. One question, for example, which Americans debated concerned the domestic consequences of entering or avoiding war; war tends to favor the executive branch and the creation of standing armies, both of which are subversive of republican government; on the other hand, fighting for one's country is the highest possible expression of civic virtue.

Third, as Hume would suggest, the balance of power system would help to encourage the growth of limited government within states because the denial of universal claims abroad would moderate absolutist claims at home. Montesquieu pointed out in his *Reflections on Universal Monarchy* that the "mediocre size" of a state alone was apt to guarantee a "government of laws." The English polemicist Charles

---

who sought to limit war by shifting to natural rights language, Butterfield uses the Christian idea of sin to argue for humility and moderation in resorting to force; see Herbert Butterfield, *Christianity, Diplomacy, and War* (London, 1953).
16. Michael Howard, *War in European History* (Oxford, 1976), 72.

Davenant, in his essay on universal monarchy, also maintained that well-founded commonwealths would be "eternal" if they could keep themselves "within a reasonable extent of territory." David Hume emphasized that the effects of commerce and of progress in the arts and sciences, which the close interaction of the European states promoted, would also encourage more liberal domestic policies.[17]

Not all modern political theorists would have agreed with Montesquieu on the desirability of mediocre size and moderate aims for the state, so reminiscent of classical theory. Machiavelli's model was Rome, the Imperial Republic, whose happiness consisted in the glory of its conquests and its dominion over others. The best state for Machiavelli was the one so organized that it could easily incorporate conquered territories, and the true statesman is the one who sees and exploits the weakness of others. The result of several states' pursuing Machiavellian aims of dominion and glory may also be described as a balance of power system however different the assumptions of national purpose are from the limited war version traced above. When the Machiavellian gains a decisive advantage, however, as Napoleon did with the creation of mass armies in Revolutionary France, his apparently moderate policies cease. Thus the balance of power which is often the outcome of the pursuit of Machiavellian aims is not the necessary outcome of such aims. Indeed, in the twentieth century doubts would arise that sovereignty-based grounds for resort to force would necessarily be more moderate, especially because of the problem of what Hans Morgenthau called "nationalistic universalism."

The suggestion being made here is that the law of nations and the balance of power emerged in their modern sense from a common opposition to religious war and to universal monarchy and is found very clearly in the work of Emmerich de Vattel, a Swiss diplomatist, whose *Law of Nations* was published in 1758. Like John Locke, whose *Two Treatises of Government* vindicated England's Glorious Revolution,

---

17. Baron de Montesquieu, "Reflexions sur la Monarchie Universelle en Europe," *Oeuvres Complètes* (Paris, 1964), 194; David Hume, "Of the Balance of Power," *Philosophical Works*, ed. T. H. Green and T. H. Grose (4 vols.; Darmstadt, 1964), II, 353–56; Davenant, *Essays Upon the Balance of Power*, 235.

Vattel's *Law of Nations* vindicated the European states system in its limited war manifestation. The principal lesson learned from the wars of religion and the Thirty Years' War was the inability of any single European state to conquer the others; instead they would have to reconcile themselves to one another's existence within a framework of equilibrium grounded in commonly accepted nonecclesiastical principles of legitimacy. Vattel's goal was to justify this lesson not simply in terms of necessity or expedience, but in terms of right. Thus he combined the universalism and categories of the just-war tradition with aspects of modern natural rights theory derived from Hobbes and praise for the balance of power system, making a new synthesis. Typical of much Enlightenment political theory, this synthesis now seems overly neat, excessively optimistic, and too easily employed as ideology. Nevertheless it is this tradition on which American statesmen have most often called to explain and defend their foreign policies; it is, moreover, possible to defend its continued relevance for present-day international relations.[18]

While many commentators have alluded to the influence of writers on the law of nations in early American thinking about international relations, few have laid it out in a systematic way.[19] The legalism and moralism of American diplomacy about which George Kennan has complained seem to have been present at its origins, but that legalism and moralism was understood to be against crusades and universal monarchy. The law of nations reflected the balance of power structure and was in turn thought to sustain the essential elements of the European system. One contention in this book is that the Americans understood this as well.

Americans in the late eighteenth century were familiar with the new science of international law and politics and were aware of the

18. Peter Butler, "Legitimacy in a States-System; Vattel's *Law of Nations*," Michael Donelan (ed.), *The Reason of States* (London, 1978), 45–63; R. J. Vincent, *Nonintervention and International Order* (Princeton, 1974).

19. See for example: Richard Cox, "Grotius," in Leo Strauss and Joseph Cropsey (eds.), *History of Political Philosophy* (Chicago, 1972), 360–69; Roger Masters, *The Nation Is Burdened* (New York, 1967); Forrest McDonald, *Alexander Hamilton: A Biography* (New York, 1979); Edward Weissbard, *The Ideology of American Foreign Policy: A Paradigm of Lockean Liberalism* (New York, 1973).

10

impact of European politics on their own lives. As American leaders sought to guide their republic safely through the perilous waters of its early years, they drew on that body of thought and experience. Chapter I examines the new science through the teaching of Vattel, on whose work the Americans relied heavily. Charles Fenwick has written that "not even the name of Grotius himself was more potent in its influence upon questions relating to international law than that of Vattel."[20] Thomas Jefferson held Vattel in high esteem; when he was persuaded to remonstrate formally to Genêt about his conduct and claims, he maintained that "We are of opinion it [United States policy] is dictated by the law of nature and the usage of nations; and this has been very materially inquired into before it was adopted as a principle of conduct. But we will not assume the exclusive right of saying what that law and usage is. Let us appeal to enlightened and disinterested judges. None is more so than Vattel."[21] Alexander Hamilton referred to Vattel as "perhaps the most accurate and approved of the writers on the laws of Nations" and regularly invoked his authority in cabinet opinions and public defenses of administration policy. Indeed, Hamilton's defense of Jay's Treaty under the pseudonym "Camillus" reads like a primer on the subject. Although Vattel was cited on specific issues—the rights of neutrals, the treatment of alien private property during war, treaty obligations, or the rights of free passage—his general teaching must be understood.[22]

Chapter II continues this analysis, with particular emphasis on Vattel's synthesis of just-war and balance of power ideas, and it includes some other writers on the subject, notably David Hume. While the intention to restrain the use of force remained the prime concern underlying the synthesis, ambiguities and unintended effects

20. Charles G. Fenwick, "The Authority of Vattel," *American Political Science Review*, VII (August, 1913), 395; see also Jessie Reeves, "The Influence of the Law of Nature Upon International Law in the United States," *American Journal of International Law*, III (July, 1909), 547–61.
21. Cited in Fenwick, "The Authority of Vattel," 410.
22. See Hamilton's "Remarks on the Treaty of Amity, Commerce, and Navigation," in Syrett and Cooke (eds.), *Hamilton Papers*, XVIII, 405–54, and "The Defense," Nos. 2, 3, 6, 14, 15, 16, 18, 20, 21, 22, 31, and 32, *ibid.*, XVIII and XIX, *passim*.

11

of Vattel's teaching made possible important disagreements about its meaning with important ramifications for the formulation of American foreign policy in the 1780s and 1790s.

Chapter III provides an overview of American foreign policy in the 1780s and 1790s; it suggests that early Americans thought in terms both of the law of nations and the balance of power and that they understood these to be mutually reinforcing. The balance of power system provided the essential bases for the law of nations; the law of nations regulated and moderated the conduct of the states within that system. But was the United States a member of that system? How far should the United States go in trying to improve it? These are issues near the heart of the foreign policy differences which emerged between Alexander Hamilton and the Federalists and Thomas Jefferson, James Madison, and the democratic-republicans. Chapters IV and V examine the approaches of these two groups to the balance of power and international law in light of their understanding of the national interest. Chapter VI makes some concluding observations on the law of nations and the balance of power as concepts in American thinking on foreign policy in light of the results of the Congress of Vienna.

CHAPTER I

Vattel on the Law of Nature and Nations

Modern political theory, on which the new science of international law and politics was founded, began with the determination to view man as he is, not as he ought to be. In this it contrasted itself with classical political theory and with revealed religion, both of which took their bearings from the highest possibilities in human nature: the capacity for reason, virtue, or devotion. Modern political theory took its bearings from the passions, that is, from what is most powerful in most men most of the time; man's true nature was most clearly seen outside of civil society. Thomas Hobbes's description of man in the state of nature, perpetually striving for power and engaged in a ceaseless war of all against all, drew the picture most starkly. Fortunately man's strongest passions, his fear of violent death and his desire for comfort, induced him to give up his natural liberty to an artificially created entity, the sovereign, in return for security. This bargain was at the heart of the social compact.

Most of Hobbes's work concerned the relationship of the individual and the sovereign, though it is possible to argue that this logic ultimately points to the establishment of a world state, which would eliminate external threats to security and keep individuals from having to give their lives in defense of the sovereign. While this result might resemble that desired by medieval advocates of world government, it has very different operating principles. Dante advocated world government because "the proper work of mankind taken as a whole is to exercise continually its entire capacity for intellectual growth," but Hobbes stressed the individual's fear of violent death as the true reason for such government. Security, not civilization, is the reason why men associate.[1]

Of more importance than possibly making a case for a world state, Hobbes provided jurists and political theorists like Wolff, Pufendorf, Locke, and Vattel, however much they disagreed with Hobbes's solution of absolute government, with the intellectual tools to vindicate the European states system on the basis of nonecclesiastical principles of legitimacy. Vitoria and Grotius had prepared the way by interpreting the just-war tradition in natural rather than divine law language. Their interpretation of natural law, however, remained heavily classical, grounded in the rational and social nature of man. Neither had they anticipated the rise of powerful monarchies capable of ignoring papal directives or the rise of the balance of power system in Europe. The situation called for a new explanation of political practice, which Hobbes's social theory seemed to provide and which Emmerich de Vattel was determined to apply to the relations of states. In Hobbes, said Vattel, "we discover the hand of a master, notwithstanding his paradoxes and detestable maxims."[2] By using social contract arguments Vattel sought to rationalize, legitimize, and ameliorate the actual practice of states in the European system. If frequency of citations to his work and extensive distribution of it are any indication of success, he was successful; the extent of his influence is acknowledged even by his most outspoken critics: "The most disheartening fact of all is that Vattel was enormously successful. The man, who as a thinker and a worker, could not hold a candle to Grotius, was so favored by fortune that the second stage of the law of nations (1770–1914 speaking roughly) may be safely called after him."[3] In this chapter Vattel, his use of Hobbes's doctrine of sover-

1. Dante, *On World Government*, 7.
2. Emmerich de Vattel, *The Law of Nations; or, Principles of the Law of Nature, Applied to the Conduct and Affairs of Nations and Sovereigns*, trans. Joseph Chitty (6th ed.; Philadelphia, 1844), sec. 7. Hereafter cited as Vattel, with references to book, chapter, and section numbers.
3. Cornelius Van Vollenhoven, *The Three Stages in the Evolution of the Law of Nations* (The Hague, 1919), 32.

14

eignty and the law of nature, and his application of these to the relations of states will be discussed. In the next, we will turn to the problem of the just war and the balance of power.

Emmerich de Vattel

Vattel was born in 1714, the son of a Reformed clergyman in the Swiss principality of Neuchâtel. His mother was the daughter of a councilor of state and treasurer general of Neuchâtel for the King of Prussia. While his two older brothers became soldiers, Vattel showed an early aptitude for law and for philosophy. In 1741 he wrote a defense of Leibnitz' system of philosophy and throughout his life he maintained contacts with the *philosophes* and cultivated the life of a thoughtful gentleman of leisure. When in 1749 the Elector of Saxony named him minister to Berne, Vattel gained greater opportunity to observe the actual practice of states close at hand. The minimal demands of his office and his philosophic bent gave him the time and the inclination to write *The Law of Nations*, which was published in 1758. Shortly afterward Augustus III of Saxony, evidently impressed by Vattel's learning, recalled him and made him privy councilor of his cabinet. Vattel apparently gave himself fully to these new duties until his death in 1767.[4]

The Law of Nations quickly achieved wide and enduring circulation. F. S. Ruddy counts twenty French editions between 1758 and 1863, ten translations in England between 1759 and 1834, eighteen translations or reprinted translations in the United States until 1872, six translations into Spanish, one into German in 1760, and one into Italian in 1805. During the hundred years after Vattel's publication Grotius went through only one more edition and one more translation.[5] Published two years after the beginning of the Seven Years' War, which culminated in the French withdrawal from North Amer-

4. Johnson, *Ideology, Reason, and Limitation of War*, 257–58. See also Fenwick, "The Authority of Vattel," 395–97, and the introduction by Albert Lapradelle in Emmerich de Vattel, *Le Droit des Gens* (Washington, D.C., 1916), *iii–iv*.
5. F. S. Ruddy, *International Law in the Enlightenment: The Background of Emmerich de Vattel's "Le Droit des Gens"* (Dobbs Ferry, N.Y., 1975), 283.

ica, the book reached America at an important stage in the development toward independence.

Vattel began his work as a condensation and systemization of the writings of Christian Wolff as they related to the law of nations. Both men in turn were influenced by the thought of Leibnitz, which refined Hobbes's thought and which addressed the problem of individual freedom and universal harmony in the world. But where Leibnitz and Wolff thought in terms of some pan-European government somewhat like the Holy Roman Empire, Vattel thought in terms of the cultural unity and political diversity which he observed in Europe. The law of nature did not require a single political unit, but if applied properly it could apply to the European system. It was that application which Vattel regarded as his principal contribution to the law of nations as a science.

Sovereignty

The first thing to be noticed about the states in Europe was their independence. They recognized no authority above their own, defined their own interests, and pursued them. Vattel argued that with certain modifications this was right and proper. Like many of Hobbes's successors, Vattel softened Hobbes's brutal account of human nature while retaining his doctrine of sovereignty based on individual desire and will. Even in the state of nature one would find "social" passions and a kind of society among men; on the basis of this sociability he located the existence of certain reciprocal rights and duties among men.[6] Thus he rejected Hobbes's extreme individualism and his account of fear as the principal basis of human society as excessive. Men came together not simply out of fear but also out of sympathy or fellow-feeling, a force which mitigated the fearful struggle for survival portrayed by Hobbes.

6. Ruddy, *International Law*, 83–84; Vattel, Preliminaries, sections 58–60. For an American exposition of this view, see Robert McCloskey (ed.), *The Works of James Wilson* (2 vols.; Cambridge, Mass., 1967), II, 228–38. Garry Wills, in *Inventing America* (Garden City, N.Y., 1978) and *Explaining America* (Garden City, N.Y., 1981), emphasizes the impact of this alternative account of human nature which he identifies with the Scottish Enlightenment on American thought.

This natural sociability was not strong enough, however, to over-come disorderly passions and private or mistaken interest and so men had recourse to political association as "the only means of securing the condition of the good, and repressing the wicked; and the law of nature itself approves this establishment."[7] Since these political asso-ciations could provide most of what men require—which Vattel de-fined as the "preservation and perfection of individuals," again set-ting himself apart from Hobbes, who referred only to preservation—political association between nations was much less necessary than association between individuals. Thus while Vattel acknowledged the unity of mankind and a universal human nature from which certain obligations and rights could be derived, he did not argue for a world state. This is much like the approach of Grotius, who rejected "world unity" or "universal monarchy" in order to urge more sociable be-havior within the community of European states.[8] Vattel took care to distance himself from Baron Wolff, whose work he greatly admired but who imagined all the nations of the world as members of a great republic "instituted by nature herself." Vattel, by contrast, admitted "no other natural society between nations than that which nature has established between mankind in general." Vattel thus prepared his reader for the propagation of different rules for states than for indi-viduals. This was in fact what Vattel himself regarded as his chief con-tribution to the study of the law of nations: with respect to nations, the law of nations must undergo some modifications "in order to ac-commodate them to the nature of the new subject [*i.e.*, states] to which they are applied."[9]

It follows from this emphasis on individual states as the primary, if not the only, agents for securing individual wants that the state's principal duty is to itself and to its members. This implies the right to "every thing that can secure it from . . . a threatening danger, and

7. Vattel, Preliminaries, sec. 11.
8. Brian Bond, "The 'Just War' in Historical Perspective," *History Today*, XVI (February, 1966), 115. R. J. Vincent, *Nonintervention and International Order*, 329–30, argues for a similar notion, describing international society as consisting of "islands of order."
9. Vattel, Preliminaries, secs. 8 and 56.

to keep at a distance whatever is capable of causing its ruin." This is not a question of immoral selfishness but of moral obligation; neither does it rule out human obligations across state lines. The fact that *all* states possess the same right to self-preservation and self-perfection limits the extent to which these rights can be invoked. The attempt of one to usurp the rights of another gives the latter the right to punish the former and secure reparation from him, which serves as the basis for Vattel's just-war doctrine to be discussed in the next chapter.[10]

Vattel treated the product of the social contract, the state, as a moral being to which rights and obligations could be attributed. In society the right of individuals to make war to restore the order of natural justice by force has been transferred to the state and is vested in the sovereign. Where medieval and Reformation political theorists had endlessly debated the question of right authority or the question of who could declare war, Vattel grounded sovereignty in the rights conferred on men by the law of nature. The authority of the church was distinctly subordinate to that of the sovereign; with Vattel, as James T. Johnson notes, the idea of the prince as the minister of God disappeared entirely.[11]

Vattel's concept of sovereignty had a strong absolutist cast. Only the sovereign had the authority to decide whether to go to war and to raise the forces necessary to conduct it. His power over his subjects obligated them to follow his lead unless it clearly harmed the common good. If he chose the wrong course of action, however, his responsibility for his subjects required that he alone must pay reparations. In direct contradiction to Grotius, Vattel asserted that the citizens and even the armed forces of a nation do not have to pay the debt for an unjust war.[12] This might make a bellicose sovereign think twice before he mobilized his armies, knowing that he would be ruined if he lost. The great separation which Vattel sought to establish, here between sovereign and subject reflected an age when wars were kings' wars and when limitations of the royal purse encouraged monarchs to seek limited political objectives and avoid decisive battles.[13]

10. *Ibid.*, Book I, Chap. 2, secs. 3–8, 20.
11. Johnson, *Ideology, Reason, and Limitation of War*, 242–43.
12. Vattel, Book III, Chap. 11, secs. 183–87.
13. Michael Howard, *War in European History*, 54–74.

18

The freedom and independence of states meant that they had a right to judge for themselves what their duty required, without being compelled to act by other states encroaching on their sovereignty. Because of this Vattel warned against the interference by one nation in the internal government of another except when invited: "It is an evident consequence of the liberty and independence of nations that all have a right to be governed as they think proper and that no state has the smallest right to interfere in the government of another."[14] Sovereignty did not depend on the form of government (except for tyranny, which posed a special problem for Vattel's system) but on the fact of self-government. Even states whose freedom of action was severely restricted by treaty arrangements with stronger states remained theoretically sovereign and entitled to appropriate treatment.

Since sovereign states had a perfect right to conduct their internal affairs as they saw fit, it followed that there exists a perfect right of equality among states. From the practical inability of one state to subdue the others—Charles V, Philip II, the Ottoman Turks, and Louis XIV had all tried and failed—a sense of equality had emerged among the European states. Unlike Hobbes, who had contended that human beings were essentially equal by virtue of their ability to kill each other, Vattel assumed an effectual equality of states from their independence and continued existence. He moved from this essentially negative kind of equality to a position which emphasized the sovereign rights and the legal equality of states, irrespective of a nation's power:

> Since men are naturally equal, and a perfect equality prevails in their rights and obligations, as equally proceeding from nature—Nations composed of men and considered as so many free persons living together in the state of nature—are naturally equal, and inherit from nature the same obligations and rights. Power or weakness does not in this respect produce any differences. A dwarf is as much a man as a giant; a small republic is no less sovereign than the most powerful kingdom.[15]

14. Vattel, Preliminaries, sec. 16.
15. *Ibid.*, sec. 18. See also McCloskey (ed.), *Works of James Wilson*, II, 241. For a critique of this doctrine see J. L. Brierly, *The Law of Nations* (Oxford, 1963), 29–91.

Vattel meant this doctrine to be a legal recognition of the political realities of the day, namely "the recognition by others of an equal claim to the right of self-help." [16] On the other hand (and Vattel himself implied this) population, natural resources, physical extent, and geographical position made some nations more powerful than others; in fact some states are more equal than others. While Vattel did not emphasize this, he acknowledged the problem by briefly imagining a rearrangement of the map of Europe to create more "naturally equal" states. He quickly laid such a solution aside as impractical and stressed instead the way alliances and coalitions could add weight to a state's power, thereby coming closer to the egalitarian ideal.

One sees here in the doctrine of the legal equality of states something of the reformist character of Vattel's work. If sovereigns acknowledged the legal equality of other states, perhaps their practice toward those other states would moderate. While powerful states presumably can take care of themselves, weak states will be able to feel more secure where their equality is acknowledged. For instance, if one accorded the Netherlands sovereign equality, one might be less likely to conquer them, especially if, as some have argued, the balance of power system itself also protects weak states. Neither of these might be enough, however; as Charles de Visscher has pointed out, "equality held no moral principle strong enough to check the appetite for domination, even when, become a 'right of equality,' it was elevated . . . to the rank of an essential attribute of the State." [17] On the other hand, persistent violation of the sovereign equality of other states has often been interpreted by other states as an indication of aggressive intent.

It is possible that this doctrine of the legal equality of states may have had the opposite effect from what Vattel intended, by exacerbating conflict rather than moderating designs on other states. Since this doctrine seems to ignore power, it may lead to the disparagement of

16. Robert W. Tucker, *The Inequality of Nations* (New York, 1977), 13.
17. Charles de Visscher, *Theory and Reality in Public International Law*, trans. P. E. Corbett (Princeton, 1957), 17. Vincent, *Nonintervention and International Order*, 43, describes the function of international law as a protector of weak states; Hans Morgenthau ascribes a similar function to the balance of power in *Politics Among Nations* (5th ed.; New York, 1973), 289–91.

power and to heightened expectations of what the legal order *qua* legal order can secure. Throughout the 1790s Hamilton and Washington were painfully aware of the weakness of the United States and called again and again for greater military expenditures and the buildup of a regular, professional army in order to give their diplomacy some weight. Hamilton in particular also wanted to encourage the nation's manufacturing sector so as to make the United States less dependent on other countries for military hardware. Jefferson and Madison, on the other hand, were deeply suspicious of armies and of manufacturing and resisted Hamilton's efforts. Yet it was Jefferson and Madison who exhibited the greatest public sensitivity to infringements of American independence and sovereign equality, particularly by the British. Their diplomatic exchanges with the British continually play on this theme: we are a sovereign nation possessive of equal rights under the law of nations and we want to be treated as such, which is after all the way you want us to treat you. This was an underlying argument in Madison's War Message in 1812, which helped to bring the United States into war with Britain and revealed how militarily weak the United States was.[18]

Throughout the discussion of sovereignty Vattel assumed, without directly stating it, that states were more or less competent to achieve those ends for which they were brought into being (which was what Hamilton was less optimistic about for the United States than was Jefferson). When discussing the right of defense Vattel remarked that a society not in a condition to repulse an aggressor "is very imperfect . . . and cannot long subsist."[19] It is in this context that he recommended that such a state somehow put itself in a position where it could resist attack, presumably through defensive alliances. This is an important qualification. Vattel's system justified on the basis of right the basic aim of the balance of power system, namely the assurance of the survival of independent states. In practice, however, this aim more accurately meant the independence of only some of the states in the system; it was all too possible for larger states to divide smaller

18. See Madison's "War Message" in James Richardson (ed.), *A Compilation of the Papers and Messages of the Presidents* (11 vols.; Washington, D.C., 1911), I, 484–90.
19. Vattel, Book I, Chap. 14, sec. 177.

ones among themselves without threatening the system as a whole, in a process Burke described as "proportional mutual aggrandisement." In such cases a Vattelian might have argued that the mere fact that a state could not avoid being annexed by others showed that it was incapable of fulfilling its obligations and deserved to be dissolved. Edward Gulick shows in his study, *Europe's Classical Balance of Power*, that some reacted to the division of Poland by Russia, Prussia, and Austria in this way; others, balance of power thinkers and international lawyers alike, thought that this violated even the minimal standards of international right conduct.[20]

The Law of Nations: Obligations

The primary obligation of the state is to itself, as is implied in the doctrine of sovereignty. There do remain, however, obligations which nations (Vattel used "state" and "nation" interchangeably) owe each other, grounded in pre-social-contract "natural" society. Unlike Hobbes, Vattel held with the Scholastics that men as men have reciprocal duties and rights based on their common humanity, but like Hobbes he held that the coming into being of sovereign states and the special character of these states modified those obligations. When James Wilson, who had played a very active part in the deliberations over the new Constitution in 1787 and who had become an associate justice on the Supreme Court of the new government, presented a series of lectures on law at the College of Pennsylvania in 1790/91, he followed Vattel closely. It is therefore not surprising that his discussion of the law of nations began with the observation that the different nature of states required "a proportional difference in the application of the law of nature."[21]

Since the question of what obligations Americans owe others as men and as citizens is one that generated and still generates disagreement, Vattel's discussion of obligations deserves a close reading. What made his observations and prescriptions seem valid was the

20. Edward V. Gulick, *Europe's Classical Balance of Power* (New York, 1955), 30–71. See also Martin Wight, "The Balance of Power," in Herbert Butterfield and Martin Wight (eds.), *Diplomatic Investigations* (London, 1966), 151–57.
21. McCloskey (ed.), *Works of James Wilson*, II, 316–17.

cultural homogeneity in Europe which helped to make the practice of war limited and temperate.

Vattel identified four kinds of obligations which may bind states: necessary (or internal), voluntary (or external), arbitrary or conventional (established by treaty), and tacit or customary (established over time by usage). The necessary law of nations is identical with the law of nature and flows directly from human nature. Men naturally seek their own preservation and perfection; these desires can be achieved only if men communicate with and assist each other; hence the establishment of the social contract. The first general law of society, therefore, is that each individual should do for others every thing which their necessities require, and which he can perform without neglecting the duty that he owes himself. When men join particular states to secure the goods which isolation does not afford them, they remain bound by this general obligation to the rest of mankind. Nations, as moral persons before the law of nations, are also bound by this same consideration which leads to the discovery of the first general law of nations: "Each individual nation is bound to contribute every thing in her power to the happiness and perfection of all the others." [22]

Here Vattel suggested that there is a great deal of congruence between state interest and the "human interest," though he did say that if a nation could not contribute to the welfare of another without doing essential injury to itself, its obligation ceased on that particular occasion. This obligation moreover ought to be considered in light of the following considerations: sovereign states are much more able to supply men's wants than are individuals, but this also suggests that states can do most of what is necessary to supply those wants without requiring assistance from other states. If a nation can assist itself, there is no need or obligation for others to help. In other words, men look to their states for the realization of their primary goals. R. J. Vincent sums this up nicely: "The goals of the security of human life, of the sanctity of contracts, and of the stability of possession of property are not pursued directly by men in international society. They are not the immediate tasks of that society, but are matters which are

22. Vattel, Preliminaries, sec. 60; McCloskey (ed.), *Works of James Wilson*, II, 317.

principally delegated to the responsibility of individual states." [23] That the experience of individuals in some of those states may fall far short of these goals is not in itself an argument for replacing it with a world state; indeed, for many in the Enlightenment the world state was synonymous with world tyranny. The balance of power system presented the possibility that at least some of humankind could experience a modicum of security and comfort; it also meant that there would be a safe haven in other states for those fleeing persecution in their own. [24]

In addition Vattel noted that the duties of a nation to itself required more circumspection and care than those of an individual to himself. As Hamilton would put it in his "Pacificus" letters, "the duty of making its own welfare the guide of its actions is much stronger upon states than upon individuals." In short, Vattel stressed and then circumscribed a nation's obligations to others though he insisted that they exist. Beginning like a world order advocate, Vattel moved to a more Augustinian position of recognizing one's limits and tending one's own garden.

This movement is reinforced by what Vattel termed the second general law of nations: "Each nation should be left in the peaceful enjoyment of that liberty which she inherits from nature." [25] This followed from the doctrine of sovereignty as well and provides one basis for the general rule of nonintervention which would be part of the Vattellian order. This law also seemed to legitimize what each European state was doing or claimed to be doing: consulting only itself about what policies to pursue. Here in effect was a natural rights ground for the principle *cujos regio, ejus religio* embodied in the Peace of Augsburg (1555) in which each prince was to determine the faith of his subjects, thereby limiting religious warfare. This Vattel granted as the proper exercise of the natural right of liberty.

Vattel's justification went beyond this to include a picture of a generally pacific international order; though it was characterized at times

23. Vincent, *Nonintervention and International Order*, 330; Vattel, Preliminaries, sec. 60, and Book II, Chap. 1, secs. 3–4.
24. Davenant, *Essays Upon the Balance of Power*, 292–93.
25. Vattel, Preliminaries, sec. 62.

by war, it was not the unremitting war of all against all which Hobbes described. In that sense Vattel is part of what Hedley Bull has termed the "Grotian tradition" in international relations theory which describes international politics as a society of states, bound together by common interests and generally accepted rules and institutions. By suggesting that states which pursue their interests properly understood can approximate the generally peaceful condition of pre-political man, Vattel reminds one of Locke and can be interpreted as an exponent of the "harmony of interests" doctrine which E. H. Carr would later attack.[26]

In addition to applying the law of nature to states in light of the special character of states, Vattel wanted to moderate the conduct of Europe's sovereigns at the very least by giving them a reputation to live up to:

> And why should we not hope still to find, among those who are at the head of affairs, some wise individuals who are convinced of this great truth, that virtue is, even for sovereigns and political bodies, the most certain road to prosperity and happiness? Here is at least one benefit to be expected from the open assertion and publication of sound maxims, which is, that even those who relish them the least are thereby laid under a necessity of keeping within some bounds, lest they should forfeit their character altogether.[27]

With respect to other nations, then, virtue seems most clearly to mean leaving others alone. Combined with the doctrine of sovereignty, this second general law of nations provides a strong basis for the establishment of some rule of nonintervention, particularly when intervention is understood as coercive interference aimed at the authority structure of a state. This in turn coincides with the biblical injunction not to do unto others what one would not have them do unto himself. Failure to abide by the peaceableness implied in the law means the possibility of prosecution of just war by the injured party.

26. Hedley Bull, *The Anarchical Society* (New York, 1977), 24–52; E. H. Carr, *The Twenty Years' Crisis* (London, 1946).
27. Vattel, Book II, Chap. 1, sec. 1.

Intervention

It is easy to see that the first law—the duty to help—and the second law—the duty to let others be—dictate potentially conflicting obligations. Substantial violations of sovereignty and even coercive interference might be justified under some claim of benevolence. Spain was notorious for having expanded its empire and wealth in the name of converting the natives to Christianity, but Vattel rejected such claims. As suggested above, he sought to establish the priority of nonintervention as a standard in international society. It was on the basis of this standard that some Americans in the nineteenth century claimed for their foreign policy a moral superiority to European foreign policies.

Vattel's preference for nonintervention, that is, the primacy of the second law over the first, is made clear in his discussion of perfect and imperfect rights. Since the primary obligation of a state is to preserve and protect itself, it has a perfect right to everything necessary to fulfill this duty. Perfect rights permit one to force compliance from those who refuse their obligations to him; imperfect rights are those rights unaccompanied by the right of compulsion and which a nation may only ask others to honor.

Imperfect rights (Vattel did not speak of imperfect duties although there seems to be no logical reason not to), those which a nation may only request observance of, include rights to the offices of humanity, commerce, passage, and embassy. According to Vattel, a state may choose not to honor another's request for trade or passage, and if so, it could not be the object of justifiable war. With imperfect rights each nation remains the judge in its own case about what best promotes its own welfare. The offices of humanity—charity—are what men owe each other as social beings formed to live in society and standing in need of assistance for their preservation and happiness. Although particular states were assumed able to provide this for their societies most of the time, famine and other such calamities gave other nations an opportunity to help if asked. On the other hand, such a request could be denied, particularly if it could be shown that fulfilling the request would be harmful to the potential benefactor. A nation could not force its humanitarianism on another state because to do so would be to violate that state's sovereignty or natural liberty. Thus Vattel rejected Spain's claim that it had a right to its American colonies on the basis of a civilizing or Christianizing duty, and he maintained that Spain had violated the Indians' natural rights. If requested, such things as the promotion of culture, education, and good law also qualified as imperfect rights under the first general law of nations, since men desire both the preservation and perfection of their beings.

Commerce was yet another way in which men supplied each other's wants and thus assisted each other, but this too was an imperfect right which only treaties may make perfect. F. S. Ruddy points out that Vattel wrote during a period of transition from mercantilism to free trade, when what had been exclusive trade areas were being opened up. Vattel defined the freedom of commerce as the right of every nation, by its natural liberty, to trade with such nations as were open to trade, but each nation was to remain the judge of the benefits to itself of engaging in trade. This right to judge could be abridged only by commercial treaty. While he held up the free trade ideal, Vattel did not treat failure to meet that standard as immoral or punishable under the law of nations. He upheld the legality of treaties which established trading rights between states to the exclusion of all others; in addition he defended the right of a state "in control of a branch of commerce, or which possesses the secret of some important manufacture, to keep to itself that source of wealth and far from imparting it to [other nations] to take measures to prevent them from taking possession of it." [28]

In his discussion of imperfect rights and the offices of humanity, Vattel included the case of a neighbor unjustly attacked by a powerful enemy which threatened to oppress it. He asserted that if one could go to the defense of such a state without exposing himself to great danger, he ought to do it, even though no formal obligation bound him to such a course. In advising this course of action Vattel implicitly defended the operation of the European balance of power system as productive of the good of all. He cited with approval the example of the alliance formed to prevent Louis XIV from taking the

28. *Ibid.*, Chaps. 1–7; Ruddy, *International Law*, 177.

Netherlands and the case of the King of Poland who saved Austria, possibly Germany, and even his own country by turning back the Turks who had laid siege to Vienna. Duty, *i.e.*, the obligation to assist others, coincided here with the sovereign's own interest in self-preservation and self-perfection because it "may be his own case to stand in need of assistance; and consequently, he is acting for the safety of his own nation in giving energy to the spirit and disposition to afford mutual aid."[29] In helping to preserve the whole, the fabric of international society, he is preserving his part as well. Significantly, however, this remained for Vattel an imperfect duty to be exercised at a state's discretion. It was for this reason that treaties were necessary, because they make perfect otherwise imperfect rights.

Vattel presented here a notable exception to the general rule of nonintervention by encouraging states to intervene on behalf of others for the sake of the balance of power. At the same time he seemed to struggle with the realization that intervening powers have their own particular interests or desires for ascendancy. Hedley Bull has remarked that "it is always erroneous to interpret international events as if international society were the sole or the dominant element." Hans Morgenthau has similarly noted that invocation of the balance of power is "one of the favored ideologies of international politics."[30] In effect what Vattel sought to sanction were wars against powers which clearly threatened the balance of power system without sanctioning wars for "mere advantage" or greed. Since it is difficult to assess correctly the relative power positions or the real intentions of states, this is a difficult distinction to put into practice. For all practical purposes Vattel left it to the various sovereigns to define it for themselves, thereby leaving open the possibility that his doctrine might sanction wars which he actually would have regarded as unjust, but which would still be moderate because of their moderate aims.

Vattel made this latitude for sovereigns clear in his discussion of the voluntary or external law of nations. Since this has an important

---

29. Vattel, Book II, Chap. 1, sec. 4.
30. Bull, *Anarchical Society*, 51; Morgenthau, *Politics Among Nations*, 212.

bearing on questions of neutrality and the just war which will be discussed later in the American context, the details and ramifications of the law will be developed there. In essence, however, the voluntary law taught states which were not party to a war to regard both sides as equally just, at least in terms of their external behavior. This law also extended to the attitude of foreign officials to tyrannical states. As contemporary just-war theorist Michael Walzer puts it, "foreign officials must act as if [tyrannical states are] legitimate, that is, must not make war against them."[31] This is an important departure from Grotius, for whom countries not concerned in the dispute are bound to distinguish between the country which inflicts punishment on a law-breaking state and the country which undergoes it, and for whom wars to vindicate natural law are just.[32] This voluntary law also prepared the way for the development of positive international law, which emphasized what states do rather than what they ought to do and for which, in the words of Quincy Wright, "attempts to distinguish just and unjust causes of war are . . . out of place."[33] As one who argued from natural rights premises, Vattel remained committed to the notion that some party in a war could be said to be just or unjust in resorting to war, but his teaching on the voluntary law of nations meant that a sovereign could make a judgment of the justice of the sides in a war without having to show it by his external actions.

One exception to the general rule of nonintervention, we have seen, was the right to intervene for the sake of a serious threat to the balance of power system. Vattel also suggested that a state may rightfully intervene on the just side in a civil war. This was partly in response to Grotius' insistence that in cases where a prince grossly vio-

31. Michael Walzer, "The Moral Standing of States: A Response to Four Critics," *Philosophy and Public Affairs*, IX (Spring, 1980), 224.
32. Vollenhoven, *Three Stages*, 11–12; H. Lauterpacht, "The Grotian Tradition in International Law," *British Yearbook of International Law* XXIII (1946), 1–53. Peter Paul Remec compares Vattel and Grotius in *The Position of the Individual in International Law* (The Hague, 1960).
33. Quincy Wright, "Changes in the Conception of War," *American Journal of International Law*, XVIII (October, 1924), 758.

lates natural law with respect to the people in his care, other princes must intervene in the name of justice to punish the wicked sovereign. Vattel rejected this justification for intervention as a violation of sovereignty and as a principle which would encourage immoderation in the practice of states.

> It is strange to hear the learned and judicious Grotius assert that a sovereign may justly take up arms to chastise nations which are guilty of enormous transgressions of the law of nature. . . . But we have shewn that men derive the right of punishment solely from their right to provide for their own safety; and consequently they cannot claim it except against those by whom they have been injured. Could it escape Grotius, that . . . his opinions open a door to all the ravages of enthusiasm and fanaticism, and furnishes ambition with numberless pretexts? [34]

Vattel sided with Vitoria and the Spanish School of Catholic jurists, which held it unlawful for Spain to subjugate American Indians on religious grounds, and Vattel extended this to wars conducted to punish sovereigns who violate their subjects' natural rights. Spain's actions in Latin America violated the Indians' sovereign rights, which Vattel so clearly insisted upon. "No state has the least right to interfere in the government of another," he declared; it is not up to a foreign power to judge the internal conduct of other nations. This all clearly follows from the doctrine of sovereignty and the independence of states. One of the charges which Hamilton would make about the French revolutionaries was that they had violated this norm. By declaring that France would defend citizens "vexed for the cause of liberty" in every country, France had invited sedition in all her neighbors. In Hamilton's view, "to assist a people in a reasonable and virtuous struggle for liberty, already begun, is both justifiable and laudable; but to incite to revolution every where, by indiscriminate offers of assistance before hand, is to invade and endanger the foundations of social tranquility." [35]

Vattel agreed that in the case of an internal struggle which had reached the level of a full-scale civil war foreign nations "may assist

34. Vattel, Book II, Chap. 1, sec. 7.
35. Alexander Hamilton, "The Stand, No. 2," in Syrett and Cooke (eds.), *Hamilton Papers*, XVIII, 394.

that one of the parties which seems to have justice on its side." Vattel acknowledged the possibility of gross tyranny in states, but maintained that it was up to the members of such states to act for themselves. The proper response to the problem Grotius raised was not outside intervention but the right of revolution.

Ironically Vattel grounded this right in the same doctrine of sovereignty which seemed so clearly to prohibit intervention; perhaps a stronger precedent existed in the actual practice of states. Since Vattel separated the sovereign and its representatives who rule, he left open the possibility that the people may change the way they wish to be ruled or that the prince could act against the interests of the people he was supposed to be serving. The concept of the state as a moral personality implied the existence of a separation between the personality and sovereignty of the state and that of the prince. In Vattel the sovereign derived its authority from those who had entered the social contract: they could overthrow a tyrannical sovereign because the ruler's right to govern was limited by the original contract, which was broken by tyranny: "The moment he attacks the Constitution of the State, the Prince breaks the contract which bound the people to him; and the people become free by the act of the sovereign and henceforth they regard him as an usurper seeking to oppress them."[36] Once this occurs, the people have a right to ask for the assistance of other nations in delivering them from their oppression. The picture presented here is one of a society at war with itself so that each of the contending parties may be considered as distinct powers which have equal rights. This was of course close to the understanding the American revolutionaries had of their own situation, though they were an English colony and not, strictly speaking, part of England itself. They had declared their independence after exhausting peaceful efforts to change British policy; they had appealed to and received aid from France and had eventually won British recognition of their independence, all more or less in accordance with Vattel's teaching.

It was in part the notion that France had intervened to support the Americans in their cause because it was a just cause (both to combat

36. Vattel, Book II, Chap. 4.

31

British oppression of her American colonies and to reduce the threat of overweening British power in the international society of states) that gave rise to the desire to express gratitude to the French by continuing to oppose the British. The experience of French aid and Vattel's teaching made Americans open to the idea that tyranny could be opposed in the name of popular sovereignty. This was certainly one argument which Jeffersonians used to justify their opposition to Jay's Treaty and the efforts by the Washington administration to patch up relations with the British. According to the Jeffersonians, the French revolutionaries espoused the cause of liberty which was a just cause and the United States was under some obligation to assist them, or at least not to assist their enemies. Both Jefferson and Hamilton understood from Vattel that this was a question of imperfect rights (though complicated by the Franco-American treaty of 1778) which meant that the United States could assist so long as it meant no harm to its own welfare. Hamilton also knew that if he could show that the French cause was itself unjust or ambiguous and if he could show that aiding the French would harm the United States, then any American obligation to the French cause would cease. By identifying all nonpopular regimes as tyrannical and unworthy of support, Jeffersonians tended to put themselves at odds with most of the rest of the world though they saw a progressive movement toward democratic principles occurring in Europe. Hamilton was less sanguine about both the benevolence of history and the applicability of republican principles in other countries. Washington's Farewell Address and the Monroe Doctrine put a high priority on the general rule of nonintervention, though demands by Americans to support the just side in a civil war (or nationalist uprisings) were heard periodically throughout the nineteenth century.

Such demands for intervention on the grounds of aiding the just cause in a civil war were not unique to Americans; in the nineteenth century the French revolutionaries, Napoleon, and Metternich made similar arguments. Democratic movements against monarchical principles by middle class people in the Netherlands, Belgium, some of the German states, and some of the Italian states gave credibility to the claims of Revolutionary France that the French were liberating

32

oppressed people in those countries. Napoleon cast himself as a champion of the freedom of the seas against British monopoly, in a generally successful effort to keep the seafaring neutrals from supporting the British. Metternich, with an entirely different view of what constituted legitimate government, regularly intervened in the civil conflicts in Europe in the first half of the nineteenth century to preserve monarchical principles of legitimacy against the principles of liberalism and nationalism. Adherence to such principles to justify intervention was, of course, closely related to the effect intervention was expected to have on the distribution of power. Intervention in civil war was one instrument in the balance of power system, yet frequent resort to such intervention would undermine the moderation which such a system was expected to promote and cast doubt on the reality of sovereignty, which was the moral and legal cornerstone on which such a system rested.[37]

37. R. R. Palmer, *The Age of the Democratic Revolution* (Princeton, 1959), 323–70; Vincent, *Nonintervention and International Order*, 332.

CHAPTER II

The Just War
and the Balance of Power

Vattel's doctrine of sovereignty and his application of the law of nature to the actions of states led him, as we have seen, to the conclusion that a balance of power system may be made more stable where the sovereign equals in a society of states are formally committed to respect one another's equality.[1] Formal adherence to a common set of ideas about the rules of conduct of these equals in their relationships also contributes to a smoother operation of the balance of power system. Vattel's discussion of the conventional law of nations, primarily treaties, and the voluntary law of nations provided the basis for such rules. The right to make treaties, make claims on other states for the performance of treaty obligations, and the proper conduct of warring and third-party states came under Vattel's review.

Treaties and the Balance of Power

Treaties, identified above as part of the arbitrary or conventional law of nations, are of two kinds: those that turn imperfect rights into perfect rights, *e.g.*, commercial treaties, friendship treaties, or agreements permitting passage, and those by which nations enter into further engagements. Through treaties the admittedly weak adherence of nations to their natural obligations may be enforced: "The most prudent nations endeavor to procure by treaties those succors and

1. Peter F. Butler, "Legitimacy in a States-System," in Donelon (ed.), *The Reason of States*, 61.

advantages which the law of nature would ensure them, if it were not rendered ineffectual by the pernicious counsel of false policy."[2]

Nations enter into treaty arrangements with others for reasons similar to those which drive men into civil society: security and comfort. Like individual men, nations may pursue misguided or short-sighted policy—threatening the security or comfort of their neighbors—which their neighbors must be wary of. This could easily be seen in the ways in which the independent European states acted to preserve that independence: they formed defensive alliances against those states which sought dominion over others. Vattel heartily endorsed the formation of alliances or confederacies which would oppose any formidable power that gave evidence of its intention to dominate Europe. Such action was legitimate because of the threat to the perfect rights of other European sovereign states and is even permissible to counter the weight of a powerful state which "by the justice and circumspection of her conduct, affords us no room to take exception to her proceedings." This observation gave Vattel a chance to praise the European balance of power system as a good in and of itself, by which modern Europe had become "a kind of republic, of which the members—each independent, but all linked together by the ties of common interests—unite for the maintenance of order and liberty." Where Europe had once consisted of political units which were detached and inward-looking, it had become a society of states governed by "the famous scheme of the political balance, or the equilibrium of power, by which is understood such a disposition of things, as that no one potentate be able absolutely to predominate, and prescribe laws to others."[3]

To the extent that the European states system promoted order and liberty it promoted the law of nature and the good of human society.

2. Vattel, Book II, Chap. 12, sec. 152.

3. *Ibid.*, Book III, Chap. 3, secs. 45–48. For similar comments see the translated excerpts of Friedrich von Gentz's "Fragments Upon the Present State of the Political Balance of Europe" in Forsyth *et al.* (eds.), *The Theory of International Relations*, 275–304. Von Gentz is not treated in the text because he wrote after the period under discussion. It is worth noting, however, that John Quincy Adams knew von Gentz and translated his essay comparing the French and American revolutions into English. See Stefan Possony (ed.), *Three Revolutions* (Chicago, 1959), 2–95.

Vattel's efforts were intended to show that the operation of the European balance of power system could conform to and promote the law of nature and nations, and he used the practice of treaty making as an example of this. He admitted that the best solution would be to make all the states in the system roughly equal in power, being aware of the problem of the inequalities of state power, but he conceded that this scheme would be impractical. Coalitions and alliances were the next best solution to the problem of unequal power and these means received Vattel's blessing. These connections would be formalized through treaties which take on the character of law. Since treaties make imperfect rights perfect, failure to fulfill treaty obligations provides justifiable grounds for the resort to war. Just as domestic societies depend on the sanctity of contracts, so the society of states, for it to remain a society, requires some rules assuring the performance of promises.

Hume and the Balance of Power

Vattel was not alone during the Enlightenment in his praise of the balance of power. David Hume, the Scottish philosopher whose political essays greatly influenced the thinking of the American founders, commended the balance of power both as a policy and as a system. While Vattel cast his praise in terms of the rights and duties of a society of states, Hume concentrated on the positive effects of the balance on European civilization. It is in fact one reason why he regarded modern politics as superior to ancient politics: "The balance of power is a secret in politics, fully known only in the present age." Hume's historical researches demonstrated that the Greeks appeared to understand the principle, yet left open the question whether they pursued it from prudence (that is, as a conscious goal) or from envy and the desire to be the leading Greek city. Whatever the motive, the effect was substantially the same: "Every prevailing power was sure to meet with a confederacy against it, and that often composed of its former friends and allies."[4]

4. David Hume, "Of Civil Liberty" and "Of the Balance of Power," in Green and Grose (eds.), *Philosophical Works*, III, 156–63 and 348–56. For discussions on the influence of the writings of Hume on the American founders see Douglass Adair,

Roman history by contrast yielded few examples of balance of power thinking, and the Romans quickly rose to world empire without ever really meeting any general combination or alliance against them. Instead of banding together to oppose Rome's imperial designs, Rome's neighbors foolishly formed alliances with Rome against others, thereby forging their own chains. That political leaders could so mistake their true interests puzzled Hume and strengthened his resolve to teach modern European statesmen where their true interests lay. He was encouraged to note the way European states had responded to the renewed threat of universal monarchy first with the Emperor Charles V of Austria and then with France under Louis XIV. Great Britain in particular received Hume's praise for understanding and following a balance of power policy, which Hume described as a necessary and just one.

Hume's defense of the balance of power as a system had both a negative "lesser of the evils" aspect and a positive "greater good" dimension. Hume greatly feared the consequences of a "universal monarchy," where religious orthodoxy enforced by a class of priests combined with absolute monarchy to oppress the world. So long as other states pursued policies which forestalled the possibility of such a condition's being realized, Hume's worst fears would be averted. Universal monarchy was so great an evil that anything else would be better; an arrangement based on the existence of several independent loci of power and authority was at least a lesser evil than universal monarchy. More than this, however, Hume looked for positive effects from a balance of power system. In what resembles some of the arguments put forward by some proponents of the American policy of contain-

---

"That Politics May Be Reduced to a Science; David Hume, James Madison, and the Tenth Federalist" and "Experience Must Be Our Only Guide: History, Democratic Theory, and the United States Constitution," in Trevor Colbourn (ed.), *Fame and the Founding Fathers: Essays by Douglass Adair* (New York, 1974), 93–106 and 107–23. For excellent critical discussions of the various meanings of "balance of power" see Inis L. Claude, Jr., *Power and International Relations* (New York, 1962), 11–37; Ernest Haas, "Balance of Power: Prescription, Concept or Propaganda?" in Arend Lipjart (ed.), *World Politics* (2d ed.; Boston, 1971), 254–68; and Herbert Butterfield, "The Balance of Power," in Butterfield and Wright (eds.), *Diplomatic Investigations*, 132–48.

ment of the Soviet Union, Hume suggested that the pursuit of balance of power policy would increase the probability that oppressive states with universalist pretensions would over time modify their goals and reform their inner nature. In praising Britain's policy of resisting French ambition, Hume allowed himself to hope "that, by maintaining the resistance for some time, the natural revolutions of human affairs, together with unforeseen events and accidents, may guard us against universal monarchy, and preserve the world from so great an evil."[5]

Hume probably hoped to contribute to this evolution with his writing. His essay on the balance of power included counsel for both the French and the British to help them see where their true interests lay. He concluded his discussion with an account of the difficulties and certain collapse which "enormous monarchies" must face, which seems directed at the French. One problem with conquering other lands and peoples was that the drive to extend dominions, as with the Roman Empire, pushed such a regime's armies farther and farther away from home to areas where those who commanded were remote from their pleasures and their fortunes. In the case of France, the "brave, faithful, and affectionate nobility" willingly fought to extend the dominions of the Bourbon monarchy but they "would never submit to languish in the garrisons of Hungary or Lithuania," far from the comforts of Paris and the locus of political power. In his essay on universal monarchy, Montesquieu had made a very similar point, though less directed at the French situation. He insisted that a large empire presupposed a despotic authority because only such a despotism could inspire the fear and exert the control necessary to administer large territories.[6]

The despotic authority would suspect the loyalty of the nobility as a class and would come to rely on mercenaries to carry on the ambitious projects of the monarchy. It went without saying that mercenaries were not actuated by patriotism and would sell their services to the highest bidder. Just as the Romans finally resorted to the use

5. Hume, "Of the Balance of Power," in Green and Grose (eds.), *Philosophical Works*, III, 353–55.
6. Baron de Montesquieu, "Reflexions sur la Monarchie Universelle en Europe," *Oeuvres Complètes*, 193.

of mercenaries, Vandals, Visigoths, and Goths who would eventually destroy Rome from within, Hume noted the presence of Croats, Tartars, Hussars, and Cossacks in the French army. He left it to the reader to conclude that as Rome had gone, so would France go unless it changed its course. Not only did the presence of other states determined to resist universal monarchy make it unlikely that France would ever achieve its ambition, but the domestic consequences of such a pursuit would probably bring down the French empire even as the Roman empire was finally brought down.[7]

This question of the size of territory and its effect on the nature of the regime lay close to the heart of the debates between the Federalists and the Anti-Federalists about the proposed constitution. With the admonitions of Montesquieu in mind the Anti-Federalists argued that a unitary government encompassing all the states, which they saw as being implicit in the Constitution, would destroy the republican liberty which they had just fought a war with Britain to preserve.[8]

Because of the advances of modern science, including political science, Hume argued that the tendency to absolutism was not inevitable. One beneficial effect of a balance of power system, considered as a system, was that it tended to promote the progress of the arts and sciences, and hence, good government. This interesting variation on the domestic consequences theme is to be found in Hume's essays "Of the Rise and Progress of the Arts and Sciences," and "Of Refinement in the Arts." In the former Hume observed that "nothing is more favorable to the rise of politeness and learning, than a number of neighboring and independent states, connected together by commerce and policy." Hume thus enlisted the balance of power on the side of progress and universal enlightenment. Just as in Greece, where "contention and debates sharpened the wits of men," modern Europe had greatly advanced learning through the interaction of a closely knit system of states. But while the ancients had praised "pov-

7. Hume, "Of the Balance of Power," in Green and Grose (eds.), *Philosophical Works*, III, 356.
8. Herbert Storing, *What the Anti-Federalists Were For* (Chicago, 1981), 15–23 and 71–76. See for example the speech made by Luther Martin in Max Farrand (ed.), *The Records of the Federal Convention of 1787* (4 vols.; New Haven, 1937), III, 180–95.

erty and rusticity, virtue and public spirit," which led to the cultivation of the martial spirit and constant war, modern Europeans had learned that commerce and refinement in the arts softened the tempers of men, making them more sociable, and tended to produce free governments. Hume here turned around Machiavelli's worry that commerce was sapping the military spirit among the Italians; rather than decry this effect, Hume cheered it, though not perhaps as much as some nineteenth-century liberals were to do. Where Machiavelli advocated enriching the state but keeping its citizens poor, Hume encouraged men to seek wealth and experience its civilizing effects. The Americans discussed these effects as well: Hamilton actively sought to encourage commercial values, though he entertained few illusions of their pacifying effects on state behavior. Jefferson dwelt on the negative effects of commerce and accused Eastern seaboard merchants and "stockjobbers" of putting their economic concerns before their patriotic duty.[9]

Hume advanced a kind of convergence theory about modern politics as a consequence of the states system: as a result of the interaction of states, monarchies and republics were coming to resemble each other. Though free governments were more conducive to the growth of commerce and the arts and sciences, monarchies in modern times had shown themselves able to learn to become civilized in the manner of free governments. The European system contributed to an exchange of ideas which indirectly led to the maintenance of a rough equality in the distribution of forces. Montesquieu captured this process when he observed:

> At present we ceaselessly imitate ourselves. Has Prince Maurice of Orange learned how to lay siege? We will get used to it. Has Cohorn [the Dutch strategist] changed his approach? We will change also. Have some made use of new kinds of weapons? Every one else will soon try them.

9. Hume, "Of the Rise and Progress of the Arts and Sciences," and "Of Refinement in the Arts," in Green and Grose (eds.), *Philosophical Works*, III, 174–97 and 305–309. For more extended discussion see Ralph Lerner, "Commerce and Character: The Anglo-American as a New Model Man," *William and Mary Quarterly*, 3rd ser., XXXVI (1979), 2–26; and James Moore, "Hume's Political Science and the Classical Republican Tradition," *Canadian Journal of Political Science*, X (1977), 809–39.

Does one state increase its troops? Or levy a new tax? It is an advertisement for the others to do the same. Finally, if Louis XIV borrows from his subjects, the English and the Dutch borrow from theirs.[10]

In checking each other's power and authority, states in a balance of power system advanced science and manners as well by subjecting each other's science and culture to vigorous analysis. Hume commented that the errors of Cartesian philosophy, to which the French were devoted, had been pointed out by philosophers of other nations and he expected the science of Newton to undergo similar testing with the truth as the final residue. In manners, the English had become aware of the "scandalous licentiousness" of their stage in comparison with that of the French, and Hume expected that awareness to improve the British theater. Thus, as a result of the operations of the European balance, Hume saw a cultural as well as political and technological convergence taking place. The balance of power system created conditions within states which permited even those regimes formerly regarded as despotic to become praiseworthy. "It may now be affirmed of civilized monarchies, what was formerly said in praise of republics alone, *that they are a government of Laws, not of Men.* They are found susceptible of order, method, and constancy. . . . Property there is secure; industry encouraged; the arts flourish; and the prince lives secure among his subjects, like a father among his children."[11]

Hume directed another part of his essay on the balance of power at the British to persuade them to refine their policy. Though the British understood the principle of the balance, Hume believed that they pursued it too recklessly. Balance of power policy is a harsh taskmaster and Hume criticized the British for pushing their wars with France beyond justice out of "obstinacy and passion." He concluded that "above half of our wars with France, and all our public debts, are owing more to our own imprudent vehemence, than to the ambition of our neighbors."[12] Here again Hume showed a concern for the do-

---

10. Montesquieu, "Reflexions," *Oeuvres Complètes*, 194. Author's translation.
11. Hume, "Of Civil Liberty," in Green and Grose (eds.), *Philosophical Works*, III, 161.
12. Hume, "Of the Balance of Power," *ibid.*, 354.

mestic consequences of foreign policy. If the problem for monarchies to avoid was overextension or unlimited conquest, the problem for republics was the ease with which they were able to create public debts to conduct wars. In antiquity governments hoarded up a supply of wealth on which they would draw during war rather than trusting to their ability to borrow once a war had begun. Modern practice was just the opposite: its policy was "to mortgage the public revenues, and to trust that posterity will pay off the incumbrances contracted by their ancestors." For once Hume approved of ancient over modern practice. "It would scarcely be more imprudent to give a prodigal son a credit in every banker's shop in London, than to impower [*sic*] a statesman to draw bills, in this manner, upon posterity." Both Hamilton and Madison would take up this theme, though for different reasons: Hamilton to argue for a sound system of public credit (with the attachment to the British commercial system which that implied) and Madison to argue that making each generation pay for its own wars would reduce the frequency of the resort to war.

For Hume judicious practice of balance of power diplomacy did not require involvement in every quarrel that involved Britain's adversary, France. Hume did not argue here from the equality of sovereigns and a general duty not to interfere—as Vattel had and as contemporary just-war theorist Michael Walzer does; he argued instead that incessant involvement in the affairs of the Continent would sap England's moral and economic strength. The British had become so sensitive to the French threat, Hume thought, that once the British were engaged in the contest, they lost all concern for themselves and their posterity and thought only of how best to harass France. To do this they had mortgaged the public revenues to pay the costs of opposition and war, but this practice could very easily prove dangerous. If the government continued to raise taxes to cover the public debt, industry would be choked off with impotence and subjection to foreign powers not far off. Nor was borrowing from abroad much of a solution, since foreign debt gave foreigners a lever to pry open and destroy the nation's integrity. Therefore, Hume held it as axiomatic that Britain should borrow from abroad only as a last resort, which in turn meant that Britain ought to refrain from involving herself in all of France's quarrels. While some have stressed the geopolitical dimension to Britain's grand strategy of "splendid isolation," Hume stressed the danger to the country's internal character which an overactive involvement in Continental politics would bring. This was counsel which the Americans too would seek to implement.[13]

Another problem attended British excess in resisting French preponderance in Europe: excess could easily produce the opposite extreme in succeeding generations "rendering us totally careless and supine with regard to the fate of Europe." This would be especially probable if national economic dislocations and maintenance of the balance were linked in the public mind. This may help to explain the rise of British pacifism after World War I. Throughout most of the nineteenth century, however, British leaders quite successfully practiced what Hume had preached. Nevertheless, Hume did not treat the axioms of the balance of power as simply self-evident; they had to be taught and remembered.[14]

Americans in their debates understood the balance of power in much the same way: as a maxim to be pursued in conducting foreign affairs and as a particular system of which they could take advantage. During the constitutional debates Madison and Hamilton sought to allay the fears of small-state advocates like Luther Martin and William Paterson that the small states would be dominated by the large states in a national government by arguing along Vattelian lines. Luther Martin had used Vattel's argument for the equality of sovereign states as one reason not to give the national government more authority. He feared that the large states would oppress the small ones. As Madison saw it, the European example provided evidence that the large states would counter each other rather than act in concert, thereby preserving the whole and indirectly protecting the small states from domination. Madison summarized his argument in his notes as follows:

> Among individuals of superior eminence and weight in society, rivalships were much more frequent than coalitions. Among independent nations preeminent over their neighbors, the same remark was verified. Carthage

13. Hume, "Of Public Credit," *ibid.*, 361–62.
14. Hume, "Of the Balance of Power," *ibid.*, 374.

and Rome tore one another to pieces instead of uniting their forces to devour the weaker nations of the earth. The Houses of Austria and France were hostile as long as they remained the greatest powers of Europe. England and France have succeeded to the preeminence and to the enmity. To this principle we owe perhaps our liberty.[15]

Not only was it probable that the larger states in the proposed union would tend to oppose each other rather than act in concert against the smaller states, as would have been true under the Articles of Confederation, small states' fears should drive them to desire the close bond envisioned in the Constitution. There the large states would be even more constricted than they were in a conventional states system. "Were the larger States formidable *singly* to their smaller neighbors? On this supposition the latter ought to wish for such a general Govt. as will operate with equal energy on the former [as on] themselves. The more lax the band, the more liberty the larger will have to avail themselves of their superior force."[16] In the twentieth century some world federalists would use similar arguments in favor of their proposal, *i.e.*, a world federation acting on persons rather than on states which would sidestep the problem of large and small states, but they overlooked the political and cultural heterogeneity of the world. Madison was much more sensitive to this problem, even within the United States. Indeed, during the Constitutional Convention he had already made it clear that the great challenge to the success of the Union would not be the conflict between large and small states but that between the northern and southern members.

Paterson of New Jersey also kept notes of the debates and in his summary of Madison's argument he included a personal note to himself (marked here in parentheses) which he believed pointed to a crucial flaw in the case Madison was trying to make:

> Mr. Madison. Have we seen the Great Powers of Europe combining to oppress the small—
> (Yes—the division of Poland.)[17]

15. Max Farrand (ed.), *The Records of the Federal Convention* (4 vols.; New Haven, 1937), I, 448.
16. *Ibid.*
17. *Ibid.*, 459.

The division of Poland among its more powerful neighbors who still remained in balance with each other showed that large states could indeed act in concert against small states. To say that the balance of power promoted the independence of states was not to say whether that included all or just some states, a point already suggested in the previous chapter. As Edward Gulick points out, there are times when the principles of the balance are not served by narrow self-interest, as when seizing the opportunity for safe conquest or annexation. At such times "balance of power theory demanded restraint, abnegation, and the denial of immediate self-interest."[18] This sounded a somewhat discordant note within the supposed harmony of interests and strikes a theme Rousseau would make good use of.

Madison implicitly recognized this in his suggestion that the United States use the European balance to its advantage. The rivalry between England and France was the principle to which "we owe perhaps our liberty." By playing one side off against the other, the United States was able to secure its independence. The balance of power in Europe created the flexibility for a relatively weak power like the United States to do this and Madison believed that the United States ought to take advantage of this situation. This belief underlay his plans to discriminate against British goods to gain diplomatic leverage with the British; such a plan would have been impossible without a potential French market for American goods. Others had suggested that the Washington administration, when it declared neutrality in the war between France and England which broke out in 1793, acted too quickly and that it should have waited to see what each side would offer in return for American neutrality. In short, many Americans recognized that the United States could take advantage of Europe's troubles. Ironically this strategy mimicked Paterson's fear, namely that states in a balance-of-power system ostensibly committed to assuring the independence of states may seek short-term advantage, short of domination, in defiance of the system's norms. Of course, the military weakness of the United States made it no threat to challenge the system as a system; of greater con-

18. Gulick, *Europe's Classical Balance of Power*, 33; Butterfield, "The Balance of Power," in Butterfield and Wight (eds.), *Diplomatic Investigations*, 140; and Kenneth Waltz, *Man, the State, and War* (New York, 1959), 159–207.

cern was the case of a Great Power which laid aside its sense of community interest for the sake of some short-term goal at the expense of the society of states.

This possibility was one reason why Vattel argued more strongly from duty than from interest. He fervently hoped that when such situations arose states would refrain from seeking immediate advantage in favor of a more far-sighted policy of general stability. (Hume had argued for something similar on the grounds of interest in the case of Britain.) Vattel insisted that one's duty to oneself meant acting on one's duty to others when the latter did not involve injury to one's perfect right. On the other hand he was not averse to arguments from advantage or interest either: "Men in power more openly sacrifice honour and honesty to present advantage [than private men]; but fortunately for mankind, it often happens that such seeming advantage proves fatal to them; and, even between sovereigns, candour and rectitude are found to be the safest policy."[19] This held true especially with respect to honoring treaties, the breach of which Vattel regarded as a violation of the other's perfect right, implying just cause for war.

The temptation which some nations might feel to renege on their commitments clearly worried Vattel, who stressed over and over again the importance of keeping one's word—even with an enemy. He insisted, for example, that a reputation for keeping one's word was a vital component of a nation's glory. Winston Churchill conceived the matter in similar terms when he wrote that "In international politics, honor leads a nation to keep its word and to act in accordance with its treaty obligations," while acknowledging that honor was a concept of political ethics, not of higher morality. Justice in international relations means rendering to each nation its due, defined as perfect rights and treaty rights; good faith means undertaking to perform one's promises. Summarized by Hamilton, Vattel's teaching was that "a policy regulated by their own interest, as far as justice and good faith permit, is, and ought to be a nation's prevailing policy."[20]

19. Vattel, Book III, Chap. 12, sec. 173.
20. Alexander Hamilton, "Pacificus, No. 4," in Syrett and Cooke (eds.), *Hamilton Papers*, XV, 86; Vattel, Book II, Chap. 5, sec. 64 and Chap. 12, secs. 163–68;

How seriously to take treaty commitments was a disputed point among Americans in the 1790s. In the early months of 1793 the Washington administration faced the problem of impending war in Europe as a result of the French Revolution. It seemed clear to most Americans that the United States ought to avoid as much involvement as possible, and yet there was the formal treaty which had been signed with France a decade earlier. Hamilton was quick to point to reasons which he thought nullified the treaty in this case, dwelling on the provisional nature of the French government, its questionable conduct in the war, and the inability of the United States to fulfill its commitment in any case. Jefferson and Madison emphasized the shared values of France and the United States and accepted French protestations that France was trying to redress the balance in Europe in order to liberalize the states system. Of the two sides, Hamilton had perhaps less faith in the efficacy of treaty commitments as an earnest of future performance, but he took seriously the commitments the United States had made. In the late 1790s he argued strenuously for a new treaty with France which would modify commitments the United States had made in 1778; whereas the United States could plead inability in 1793, the nation would not always be so weak and could not expect to use that justification reasonably to wriggle out of treaty commitments in the future.[21]

The Balance of Power and the Just War

Throughout his work Vattel held it an invariable truth that justice is "inseparable from sound policy" and "a branch of justice is never advantageous." It followed from this that Vattel regarded war for "mere advantage" unjust. Although international lawyers and international relations theorists have frequently stressed or advocated the separation of the balance of power from law and morality, Vattel did not. As already noted, Vattel frequently invoked "right," "duty," and "justice" to shore up imperfections in the balance of power system with

---

Churchill cited in Kenneth W. Thompson, *The President and the Public Philosophy* (Baton Rouge, 1981), 41.
21. Hamilton to James McHenry, April 29, 1797, in Syrett and Cooke (eds.), *Hamilton Papers*, XXVI, 65–66.

respect to the integrity of states and to the making of treaties. Those discussions pointed to the central question of Vattel's work: when was war justified? Vattel seemed convinced that a just-war theory could be worked out in spite of a variety of objections that could be made about any such theory.

Because Vattel wanted to explain the European system at the level of right, he had to offer some standard of conduct (the law of nature and nations) the violation of which was unjust and punishable. He thus defined war as "that state in which we prosecute our right by force." This followed logically from the doctrines of sovereignty and perfect rights. The foundation of every just war was injury, either committed or threatened.

"And, in order to determine what is to be considered as an injury, we must be acquainted with a nation's rights, properly so called, that is to say, her perfect rights. . . . Whatever strikes at these rights is an injury, and a just cause of war." The objects of a lawful war are (1) to recover what belongs to us, (2) to provide for our future safety by punishing the offender, and (3) to defend ourselves from injury. The first two are the essentials of just offensive war and the third, just defensive war.[22]

Besides the fact that some theory of just war must follow from Vattel's moral philosophy, it seems meant to make wars less frequent. The consequences of war are such that it should never be undertaken without the weightiest of reasons. Vattel admitted that sovereigns would use the above categories as pretexts "alleged as justificatory which are so only in appearance, or which are even absolutely destitute of all foundations." Nevertheless he seemed to hope that the exercise of justification would induce some moderation in the offending party: "Pretexts are at least a homage which unjust men pay to justice. He who screens himself with them shows that he still retains some sense of shame. He does not openly trample on what is most sacred in human society: he tacitly acknowledges that a flagrant injustice merits the indignation of all mankind." One reason for the appearance of declarations of war may be traced to the desire which

22. Vattel, Book III, Chaps. 1–3.

even the least scrupulous sovereigns have to be thought just, equitable, and lovers of peace.[23]

Shame, said Hobbes, is a sign of the love of good reputation, and Vattel implied that it was a passion which could restrain men; to put it another way, hypocrites by their very hypocrisy remain within the bounds of human society. Michael Walzer, who uses hypocrisy as evidence of a moral sense even in war, puts it this way: "Wherever we find hypocrisy, we also find moral knowledge."[24]

Vattel condemned wars undertaken "merely from motives of advantage" and those conducted by nations "who seem to delight in the ravages of war, who spread it on all sides, without reasons or pretexts." These nations are "monsters" and "unworthy the name of men" who should be considered as "enemies to the human race." Vattel cited the tribes which destroyed the Roman Empire, Genghis Khan, Tamerlane, and Attila in this connection. Later he mentioned the Barbary pirates, against whom Thomas Jefferson was to conduct hostilities, as people outside the pale of civilized conduct and worthy of punishment.[25]

Vattel was troubled by the problem of mixed motives, *i.e.*, where a just cause exists, but where the main or sole reason for the resort to war is advantage. Such conduct cannot be condemned as unjust, but Vattel recognized that it sacrificed the traditional just-war criterion of right intention: "He who, having in reality just ground for taking up arms, is nevertheless solely actuated by interested views in resorting to hostilities, cannot indeed be charged with injustice, but he betrays a vicious disposition."[26] This points up one tension between just-war and balance of power thinking: whether to focus on the frequency or on the moderation of war. The case for making mundane goods the

23. *Ibid.*, Chap. 3, sec. 32.
24. Walzer, *Just and Unjust Wars*, 19–20; Vattel, Book III, Chap. 3, sec. 34.
25. For Jefferson's views on the Barbary pirates see the editorial note, "Jefferson's Proposed Concert of Powers Against the Barbary States," in Julian Boyd *et al.* (eds.), *The Papers of Thomas Jefferson* (20 vols.; Princeton, 1950–   ), X, 560–66, and Reginald Stuart, *The Half-Way Pacifist: Thomas Jefferson's View of War* (Toronto, 1978), 14–17.
26. Vattel, Book III, Chap. 3, sec. 33.

objects of war lies in the conviction that limited aims and means will tend to produce temperate wars, though they may occur as frequently as sovereigns choose. To focus on the frequency of war is to require a closer examination of the reasons for the resort to war and perhaps some restrictions on sovereigns. Jeffersonians complained that monarchs, unrestricted by the voice of the people, resorted to war far too frequently and on the most flimsy of excuses. That was one reason why they maintained that popular governments were more pacific in nature than monarchies.

That sovereigns use pretexts means that it is possible to distinguish the justifications for war and the motives for war. The former attempt to show the justice of a war; the latter determine the expedience for the sovereign in exercising his claimed right. This was a distinction which Hamilton, in particular, adhered to in his written cabinet opinions and its presence there provides good evidence that Hamilton read Vattel closely. In his opinion on the Nootka Sound crisis, which raised the possibility that the British would ask permission from the United States to march through American territory to oppose and confront the Spanish in Louisiana and would claim the right of free passage as their legal basis, Hamilton wrote that it would not be appropriate to refuse the British request by citing the effects British possession of Louisiana would have on inhabitants of the western territories and on the Atlantic trade of the United States. These reasons were motives, not justifications, and so would be inappropriate in the American response.[27]

Vattel divided motive into two classes: proper and vicious. So long as a sovereign acts out of concern for the advantage and safety of its citizens, it acts from a proper motive; if, on the other hand, the sovereign acts out of the violence of its passions it acts viciously, as in the "arrogant desire of command, the ostentation of power, the thirst of riches, the avidity of conquest, hatred, and revenge." Giving way to these passions may satisfy the sovereign's lust for a time, but Vattel doubted that this could lead to real happiness for a state. "Though an unjust war for a time may enrich a state, and extend her frontiers, it

27. "Nootka Sound Opinion," in Syrett and Cooke (eds.) *Hamilton Papers*, VII, 36–37.

renders her odious to other nations, and exposes her to the danger of being crushed by them. Besides, do opulence and extent of dominion always constitute the happiness of states?"[28] American critics of the Mexican War, the conquest of the Philippines, and the Vietnam War would reiterate this theme (though without the fear of being crushed by others for success in these unjust enterprises).

Even if the sovereign is reasonably confident that he has a just cause, he must also consider the benefits war might bring to his state; these benefits appear in the context of the consideration of the proper motives for war. Vattel, like Grotius, Pufendorf, and Wolff before him, urged in his just-war theory the criterion of a cost-benefit calculation which is the core of prudence: "In order to be justifiable in taking up arms it is necessary—1. That we have a just cause for complaint. 2. That a reasonable satisfaction has been denied us. 3. The ruler of the nation, as we have observed, ought maturely to consider whether it be for the advantage of the state to prosecute its right by force of arms." This holds true for prospective allies as well: "If there be question of contracting an alliance with a nation already engaged in a war, or on the point of engaging in one, two things are to be consulted: 1. The justice of that nation's quarrel. 2. The welfare of the state." Indeed, on the second point Vattel indicated that inability or possible self-destruction negate treaty obligations, as do an ally's folly or injustice (points which Hamilton and John Quincy Adams both made in their discussions of the Franco-American alliance). The idea of proportionality in considering the resort to war requires thought about the impact of the war in question upon one's own society and the interest of the society the war is intended to serve. In just-war language, the evil produced by the war must not be greater than the good done or the evil averted by it. Vattel's chapter on the just causes of war began with a reminder to its readers of the high costs of war so that "whoever considers its terrible effects, its destructive and unhappy consequences, will readily agree that it should never be undertaken without the most cogent reasons."[29]

28. Vattel, Book III, Chap. 3, sec. 33.
29. *Ibid.*, Chap. 6, sec. 85; "Americanus, No. 1," in Syrett and Cooke (eds.), *Hamilton Papers*, XV, 669–78.

While just-war and balance of power advocates agree on the importance of proportionality in considering the resort to war, they do often diverge on the question of what to count when doing the calculation. Just-war theorists tend to define the criteria morally while balance of power theorists tend to emphasize material criteria; balance of power theorists also tend to put a higher premium on the idea of success. This distinction will appear again in discussion of proportionality and economy of force in the *jus in bello*. The assertion that a nation's commitments ought to be brought into line with its capabilities may sometimes mean an enlargement of the goals of a state's foreign policy (the United States at the beginning of the twentieth century) and sometimes mean a reduction of commitments (the United States in the late 1960s and early 1970s). The underlying principle is that the state ought to devote itself to what it can reasonably expect to achieve given limited resources and the potential opposition of other states. Just-war theorists, on the other hand, tend to stress with John Courtney Murray that in calculating proportionality emphasis must be on the realities of the moral order, and not merely on two sets of material damage and loss. The cost of a war which necessarily involves indiscriminate bombing of civilian targets includes the loss of the principle of noncombatant immunity. Failure to oppose the encroachment upon neutral rights by a tyrannical power means that that principle is sacrificed at the cost of maintaining peace.

> There are greater evils than the physical death and destruction wrought in war. And there are human goods of so high an order that immense sacrifices may have to be borne in their defense. . . . The tradition of reason has always maintained that the highest value in society is the inviolability of the order of rights and justice. If this order disintegrates or is successfully defied, society is injured in its most vital structure and end.[30]

The criterion of proportionality applies more clearly in offensive than defensive wars, as does the difference in emphasis suggested above. Self-defense may be urged as a right to self-preservation or as a struggle to preserve the values which make the nation a nation, but

30. John Courtney Murray, *We Hold These Truths* (Garden City, N.J., 1964), 249.

these arguments reinforce each other. Similarly coalitions may be formed against a threat to the balance of power system on the basis of the right of self-preservation or in order to preserve the values of international society. The real divergence becomes evident in disputes which do not threaten the existence of states (as in the colonial wars of the nineteenth century) or the states system as a whole (as in the case of Poland).

To summarize, Vattel's just-war theory includes thus far the following criteria, as compared with those of the classical theory. Vattel resolved the question of right authority with Hobbes's doctrine of sovereignty and the state, and thus he put aside the questions of church and state that had plagued medieval theologians and the issue of public and private war that Grotius had discussed. Nationalist and class interpretations of sovereignty which arose in the nineteenth century, however, would reopen the problem. Next, Vattel emphasized just cause, grounded in injury, which legitimized the resort to defensive and, in some cases, offensive war. Even if a state has just cause, it ought to weigh the costs and benefits of exercising its right to war. The classic emphasis on right intention tended to disappear or be made subordinate, so that war undertaken with vicious motives but with just cause was tolerated by Vattel. War itself should be a last resort after other attempts to gain redress have failed and it should be accompanied by a declaration of war. Indeed, the declaration of war was, for Vattel, a final step short of the actual outbreak of hostilities, given as an indication of the seriousness of the situation. It provided one last opportunity for the adversaries to come to terms before a final break. More recently the opposite argument has replaced this view: now it is said that declarations of war ought to be avoided because they tend to prevent any possible turning back from hostilities. This shift may be due in part to the effort to "outlaw" war in the twentieth century, which goes far beyond anything Vattel envisioned.

One pretext which Vattel refused to admit as legitimate in the law of nations concerned the propagation of religion. Missionary work conducted through "mild and lawful means" was permissible, but the principle of nonintervention in the affairs of other governments delegitimized crusades. Vitoria had insisted that the Indians in South America had to receive Spanish missionaries on the basis of the principle of free passage; Vattel would have nothing to do with this argument, though he retained the notion of free passage as an imperfect right. Even "when a religion is persecuted in one country, foreign nations who profess it may intercede for their brethren; but this is all they can lawfully do."[31] Only in the most extreme cases, when the issue is not simply religious intolerance but manifest tyranny, did Vattel countenance outside intervention and that only when one group in a virtual civil war asks for help. As a rule the internal character of another regime is unacceptable as a basis for a justifiable foreign policy. This rule reflected a European system, epitomized by Cardinal Richelieu's alliance with the German Protestants against Spain, where statesmen made alliances with other states irrespective of the internal character of those other states. Here Vattel's just-war theory reinforced the workings of the moderate European balance of power system.

Vattel was aware of a number of objections or problems which his (or any) just-war theory raised. In particular, he addressed the following: Can there be justice on both sides of a war? What ought to be done about a state which increases in power but does not actually injure its neighbors? Doesn't the claim of justice decrease moderation in warfare? Vattel's considerations of these questions prepared the way for his discussion of the voluntary law of nations and the questions of just conduct in war.

To the problem of ambiguous or difficult cases where both sides claim justice, Vattel maintained the classic view that by the rules of logic war cannot be just on both sides. Warring parties are like two individuals disputing the truth of a proposition "and it is impossible that two contrary sentiments should be true at the same time." Like Grotius and Vitoria, Vattel held that it was possible for states to be innocent because of ignorance, though they were guilty, speaking strictly. Vitoria had invoked the concept of "invincible ignorance" to argue against the possibility of justifying war by referring to true religion as the Spanish had done in South America. Invincible ignorance in this case stood for "the state of nature" in which the Indians lived: they could not know the true religion. But the same concept

31. Vattel, Book II, Chap. 4, sec. 62.

54

could be applied to European nations when rival princes made claims and counterclaims which could not be sorted out even by the wisest and most objective of third-party observers.[32] John B. Wolf in his study on the European balance of power system notes, for example, that every crown in eighteenth-century Europe was composed of previous dynastic combinations. The Spanish crown was actually some twenty-odd crowns joined together by the accidents of marriage and inheritance; the same was true for the crowns of the British Isles, France, Poland, Hungary, the Hapsburgs, and the Hohenzollerns. Consequently, in the War of the Spanish Succession right was very hard to determine: "There were three princes who could claim the right of succession: Louis, the Grand Dauphin of France, or one of his sons; the Archduke Charles whose elder brother Joseph had become king of Hungary and of the Romans and the little electoral prince Joseph Ferdinand of Bavaria."[33]

The possibility of unknowing guilt was also raised in part to encourage moderation on two sides of a conflict, reasoning as follows: "When neither side can be unqualifiedly certain of the justice of its cause, it is that much more bound to observe scrupulously the limits set in the *jus in bello*." In such cases Vattel, like his predecessors, advised the antagonists to try to resolve their differences short of war through compromise, arbitration, third-party mediation, single combat (in Grotius), or conferences. From Vitoria's doctrine of invincible ignorance came the broader conception of "simultaneous ostensible justice" (the phrase is James T. Johnson's), which contributed to an emphasis on a procedural view of just-war justification, to an increased concern with *jus in bello* over *jus ad bellum*, and to the legal possibility of neutrality.[34]

A second problem presented by Vattel's just-war theory came from the practice of the balance of power. Vattel asked himself "whether the aggrandisement of a neighboring power, by whom a nation fears

32. Johnson, *Just War Tradition*, 98; Vattel, Book III, Chap. 3, sec. 39; and Grotius, Book II, Chap. 23.
33. John B. Wolf, *Toward a European Balance of Power, 1620–1715* (Chicago, 1970), 125.
34. James T. Johnson, "Toward Reconstructing the *Jus Ad Bellum*," *Monist*, LVII (October, 1973), 461–88.

she may one day be crushed, be a sufficient reason for making war against him." For the power politician the answer is probably yes, but for Vattel "an increase of power cannot, alone and of itself, give any one a right to take up arms in order to oppose it." It may be that such a state has increased its power within the spirit and the law of the law of nations; Vattel doubted the probability of such cases, but he admitted the possibility and tried to address it.

The states who fear the growing power of such a neighbor are not without recourse. First, as mentioned earlier, Vattel counseled the creation of alliances and confederacies which would be able to oppose such a power without having to initiate war against it. Second, Vattel distinguished intention and capability. "Now, power alone does not threaten an injury; it must be accompanied by the will." Capability is a military calculus, while intention is more political, and it is the latter which merits close attention in Vattel's opinion. Nevertheless, he admitted that though logically separable, power and the inclination to use it usually go together; he used a mathematical analogy to suggest that the greater the probability of danger from a large state, the more justified the other or others are in entering preventive war against it. While this is especially so in the case of a nation manifestly ambitious, a degree of caution should pertain as well with respect to the large apparently peaceful state as well. In the case of a state which suddenly, in the midst of peace, erects fortresses on its borders, augments its troops, fills its magazines, and generally makes preparation for war, Vattel did not automatically sanction a preemptive strike to prevent injury (just wars being contingent on injuries received), but he did make his counsel subject to an analysis of that state's intentions. Such an arms buildup required prudence and vigilance, but not necessarily war.[35]

It is possible, too, that Vattel's retention of offensive war to avenge injury could play into the hands of an aggressive state. Napoleon justified his course in Europe partially on the grounds that he was defending neutral rights from British encroachments and that he was

---

35. Vattel, Book III, Chap. 3, sec. 42 and 50; see also Alfred Vagts and Detlev Vagts, "The Balance of Power in International Law: A History of an Idea," *American Journal of International Law*, LXXIII (October, 1979), 555–80.

going to redress the harm done the Poles by the partitioning of their country. Presumably Vattel would have argued, as von Gentz did, that the means—domination of Europe and destruction of the society of states—worked in direct opposition to the proposed ends.

Another solution to this problem, which became popular in the twentieth century, is to outlaw just offensive war. In contemporary international law and Catholic just-war teaching, self-defense is sanctioned but first resort to force is condemned. Pope Paul V, for example, refused to admit that any nation ever had the right to initiate war for whatever cause. One result of this has been to make all wars wars of self-defense, thereby stretching the right of self-defense beyond recognition and making declarations of war obsolete. Second, as James T. Johnson argues, this leads to an excessively narrow definition of aggression as first use of force, where that definition ignores the practical problem of one side provoking the other to attack. "The reduction of the concept of *jus ad bellum* to the simple outlawry of first strikes and the legitimation of all second strikes may make the task of adjudication much easier—indeed, even automatic—yet it opens the possibility of highly provocative and damaging acts short of first armed attack on the part of nations wishing to draw others into war." Third, contemporary doctrine may (understandably) be too preoccupied with the problem of nuclear war and forget that conventional war remains a practical possibility in many parts of the world. There seem to be times when justice and/or the balance of power system may be served by offensive war.[36]

The objection that just-war claims hamper moderation is one which concerned Vattel a great deal, particularly for the making of peace. Presumably in wars fought simply and exclusively for material advantage compromise to conclude a conflict is fairly easy to achieve once the relative distribution of forces is evident and the goods may be divided accordingly. To add the moral dimension would probably make the parties more rigid in their demands. Even though Vattel's theory differed from the religious accounts of war in conceiving in-

36. Johnson, "Reconstructing the *Jus Ad Bellum*," 475; Walzer, *Just and Unjust Wars*, 74–85; and Vagts and Vagts, "The Balance of Power in International Law," 555.

jury in finite terms—reparable within the limits of the law of nations—and with due regard for proportionality—the means of war commensurate with its purpose which is to bring an adversary to reason and not to destroy him—,Vattel nevertheless conceded that claims of justice and injustice may create obstacles in concluding a war. Thus: "There would be no stability in the affairs of mankind, no safety in trading with nations engaged in war, if we were allowed to a distinction between a just and an unjust war, so as to attribute lawful effects to the one, which we denied to the other. It would open a door to endless discussions and quarrels." Vattel's concern here was with how the parties' gains are to be treated: these are the "external effects" of war. It may be that a warring party acquires territory using means in excess of what is strictly appropriate according to the norms of proportionality. Right goes hand in hand with necessity and the exigency of the case, but Vattel admitted that it is very difficult to form a precise judgment of what the present case requires, especially because, according to the necessary law of nations, sovereigns remain the judges of what the situation requires.[37]

Practical examples of this problem may be found in all wars including the American Revolution. Thomas Jefferson, for example, accused the British of injustice in the conduct of their war against the Americans for exciting the Indians against the Americans, for encouraging slave insurrections, for sending American prisoners to the East Indies and keeping them on half rations or killing them in British prisonships, for murdering unarmed individuals, and for slaughtering those who had asked for quarter. As secretary of state, Jefferson repeated some of these charges in a letter to the British envoy to America, George Hammond, in response to Hammond's charges of misconduct. After offering some examples of British misconduct, however, Jefferson concluded by citing Vattel to the effect that the state in which things are found at the moment a treaty is enacted is to be considered the proper starting point for the discussion of grievances. Some American grievances had made their way into the peace

37. Vattel, Book III, Chap. 13, sec. 195 and Chap. 8, sec. 137. For a modern critique of the vagueness and hence the malleability of proportionality in the *jus in bello* see Robert Osgood and Robert W. Tucker, *Force, Order, and Justice* (Baltimore, 1967), 300–302.

treaty and Jefferson pressed the American case on those points, but dropped the grievances which were not a part of the treaty.[38]

How are other states to regard the gains and losses of war, since there is no impartial judge of a nation's conduct in war? This brought Vattel on to what he termed the "voluntary law of nations," which has for its end the safety and advantage of mankind (in this its end is identical with that of the necessary law of nations) but which softens the distinctions of right that operate in a just war. One should feel bound oneself as a sovereign to the necessary law of nations, but one should apply a more lenient standard to the conduct of others. The benefit of the voluntary law of nations is that it "tolerates what cannot be avoided without introducing greater evils." That greater evil would be the institution of some supranational agency charged with assessing the motives and justice of a sovereign's cause; such an agency would, by definition, mean a restriction of state sovereignty, and raised for Vattel the spectacle of universal empire. To charges by Lauterpacht and Vollenhoven that Vattel permitted the sovereign to do anything he wanted without reference to natural law, Vattel might have replied: No, the sovereign is still bound in conscience by the natural law but it is not up to other sovereigns to judge with authority whether he has conformed to that law or not. The practical effect, however, of Vattel's doctrine may come close to that pictured by Lauterpacht and Vollenhoven, because there is no enforcement mechanism to make the sovereign comply with his conscience.[39]

There are two general rules in the voluntary law: first, regular war (as distinct from war for religion or for universal empire), as to its effects, is to be accounted just on both sides. This is necessary to in-

38. "Comments on Soule's *Histoires*," in Boyd *et al.* (eds.), *Jefferson Papers*, X, 370; Jefferson to George Hammond, May 29, 1792, in Paul L. Ford (ed.), *The Works of Thomas Jefferson* (12 vols.; New York, 1905), VII, 12–14. For a review of the adherence to the law of land warfare during the American Revolution see Martin Clancy, "Rules of Land Warfare During the War of the American Revolution," *Yearbook of World Polity*, II (1962), 203–317. Clancy is more sympathetic than Jefferson to the problem the British faced in trying to distinguish combatants and noncombatants.

39. Vattel, Book II, Chap. 1, sec. 189 and Book III, Chap. 13, sec. 196; Lauterpacht, "The Grotian Tradition," 40–53; Vollenhoven, *The Three Stages of the Evolution of the Law of Nations*.

troduce some order, regularity, and boundaries to the calamity of war, thereby leaving the door open for the return of peace. In other words, what gains or losses a nation sustains in war are to be regarded as justly gotten whatever the merits of a nation's original cause. That is how Friedrich von Gentz, writing on the balance of power in 1806, responded to Napoleon's claim that France had a right to punish Prussia, Russia, and Austria for their unjust partition of Poland. Gentz agreed that the partition was wrong according to the public law of Europe and destructive of the basis of the European balance system: "The cause of public justice was on all hands abandoned and betrayed." Nevertheless, Gentz could not sanction, and even condemned, the revival of Poland's case, in words reminiscent of Vattel's. "But we have at last suffered enough; ruins heaped on ruins, disaster on disaster, and a mass of violence and crime, such as no age ever witnessed, has covered up that old act of injustice. To bring it again forward to view, for the sake of grounding upon it new usurpations, is a pretension so repulsive in its nature, that all Europe must unite in raising its voice against it." [40]

The second general rule of the voluntary law followed from the first: since both sides in a regular war are held to be equally just, whatever is permitted to one side in the state of war is permitted also to the other. This rule would be of particular interest to neutral powers, since it provided them with the legal right to trade with both sides without being accused of taking sides. It was an extension of "simultaneous ostensible justice" to almost all wars, though Vattel claimed that the voluntary law did not extend "real" rights to one fighting an unjust war, "but merely entitles him to the benefit of the external effect of the law, and to impunity among mankind." This question of external right does not free sovereigns from their responsibility to pursue only just wars. Vattel did not want to appear to sanction unjust wars, yet once war had begun he was anxious to moderate

40. Gentz, "Fragments on the Political Balance of Europe," in Forsyth *et al.* (eds.), *The Theory of International Relations*, 291; Vattel, Book III, Chap. 12, sec. 190. Vattel's position makes him a leading member of a group whose attitude Inis Claude, Jr., has described as finding it a "useful pretense" to hold that all resorts to war are permissible. See Inis Claude, Jr., "Just Wars: Doctrines and Institutions," *Political Science Quarterly*, XCV (Spring, 1980), 83–96.

its conduct and limit its spread. Grotius had labeled these rules arbitrary and dependent on the consent of nations, but Vattel grounded them in the necessary law of nations by arguing that both have the same purpose: to promote human happiness and perfection.[41]

Just Conduct in War

Vattel's exposition of the law of nations reflected a continuing effort within the just-war tradition to restrain both the resort to war and the conduct of war. The delegitimization of a religion-based *jus ad bellum* and the development of the legal position of simultaneous ostensible justice evident in Vitoria, Grotius, and Vattel ought to be understood as part of that effort. In addition Vattel's doctrines of sovereignty, the legal equality of states (however unequal their power) within a balance of power system, and the voluntary law of nations provided legal limitations on the extent of a state's war aims. The tradition of *raison d'état* and its concern with the preservation and augmentation of state power provided another important rationale for some limitations as well.

Shakespeare recognized and treated this question in his play about the just war, *Henry V*. Having established a just claim to the throne of France and yet being rebuffed by France, England's King Henry V resorts to just war against France. A key target in the English campaign is the French port of Harfleur, to which the English lay siege. After some time, during which the English feel that they have demonstrated an eventual victory, Henry warns the governor of Harfleur to surrender or take the consequences of continued foolish resistance; although a leader wishes his army to be restrained, warfare requires passions antithetical to restraint. If the governor does not surrender

> The gates of mercy shall be all shut up,
> And the fleshed soldier, rough and hard of heart,
> In liberty of bloody hand shall range
> With conscience wide as hell, mowing like grass
> Your fresh fair virgins and your flow'ring infants

41. Vattel, Book III, Chap. 12, secs. 191–92.

· ·
Therefore, you men of Harfleur
Take pity of your town and your people
Whiles yet the cool and temperate wind of grace
O'erblows the filthy and contagious clouds
Of heady murder, spoil, and villany.[42]

Just-war theorists, in spite of this problem of political psychology, have resisted the notion that "war is hell" and must be resisted at all cost. They have maintained the view that war, like any other human activity, can be a rule-governed activity. James Childress, an exponent of this approach, summarizes it as follows: "Some ways of waging war are more compatible than others with the overridden *prima facie* duties not to injure or kill others. War can be more or less humane and civilized. War and politics, or peace, are not two totally separate realms or periods. Both are subject to moral principles and rules, and indeed, to many of the same principles and rules."[43] Usually just-war theorists have defined these principles as "proportionality" and "discrimination," both of which are found in Vattel's account of the *jus in bello* to which we now turn.

Mention has already been made of the principle of proportionality in the *jus in bello* in connection with the voluntary law of nations. In its essence this principle teaches that because one's enemies are also men, one should employ the minimum amount of force necessary to bring them to reason. Vattel maintained that "the lawfulness of the end does not give us a real right to any thing further than barely the means necessary for the attainment of that end. Whatever we do beyond that, is reprobated by the law of nature, is faulty, and condemnable at the tribunal of conscience." The application of this principle varies according to the circumstances and the situation. Right goes hand in hand with necessity and the exigency of the case, but never exceeds them. The vagueness of this principle is notorious, though it does resemble the military principle of "economy of force." Once an

42. William Shakespeare, *Henry V*, Act III, Scene 3, lines 10–14 and 27–32. Michael Howard makes the same point, albeit more prosaically, in his essay "*Temperamenta Belli*: Can War be Controlled?" in Michael Howard (ed.), *Restraints on War* (Oxford, 1979), 1–15.
43. Childress, "Just-War Theories," 433–34.

enemy has asked for quarter or surrendered, there is no moral justification to kill him since he has given up his cause. Nor is there a military rationale for continued killing in such cases, either because the military goal has been achieved or because an army's leaders want to conserve their arms and energy in order to achieve it.

Vattel also counseled a kind of proportionality with respect to needless violence directed toward the lands and cities of the enemy. He cited as especially savage the uprooting of vines and the cutting down of fruit trees. Such actions desolate a country for many years to come and go far beyond any military necessity: "Such a conduct is not dictated by prudence, but by hatred and fury." He specifically disallowed the bombardment, burning, spoliation, or other defacement of "fine edifices" that "do honour to human society, and do not contribute to the enemy's power." He also indicted bombardments of cities with red-hot cannon balls, which tended to start fires indiscriminately wherever they landed.[44]

In making these judgments Vattel drew on the moral experience of his time. Louis XIV had not only threatened Europe with universal monarchy, but had become notorious for exceeding accepted *jus in bello* standards. As told by John Wolf, the French thought it necessary, in order to fortify recently taken positions on the Rhine, to devastate the Rhineland so as to make it difficult for an enemy to establish any kind of beachhead against the French fortifications. The king ordered his soldiers to destroy all the chateaux, villages, towns, and cities that could be used by an enemy army in a band of German territory about fifty miles deep. Many of the nobleman officers refused to carry out these orders or did so half-heartedly so that the destruction, though considerable, was not on the scale envisioned by the king. Nevertheless, "this was the fateful decision that was to give the French a reputation as bad as one acquired by the Huns when they penetrated Europe centuries before." While Vattel could not force leaders to refrain from such tactics, he endeavored to construct a heavy presumption against their use.[45]

Just-war theorists, in view of the variability of proportionality in

44. Vattel, Book III, Chap. 8, sec. 137 and Chap. 9, secs. 157, 166–69.
45. Wolf, *Toward a European Balance of Power*, 102–103.

the *jus in bello*, have more often stressed the principle of discrimination or noncombatant immunity as another way to limit the effects of war. Vattel held that by the doctrine of sovereignty when a sovereign declared war against another, it was understood that the whole nation declared war. This made all the subjects of the one nation enemies to all the subjects of the other. This conclusion did not obviate the necessity of discrimination; though women, children, the sick, and elderly are to be considered enemies, it did not follow that they were to be treated in the same way as men who bear arms or those who led the nation. Not all enemies could be said to be engaged in a direct threat to oneself or to one's friends. When detailing the duties of the sovereign to defend the state Vattel had written that everyone not "incapable of handling arms, or supporting the fatigues of war," or performing services "useful and necessary to society" was subject to becoming a soldier. The other side of this was that all who are too weak or who perform nonthreatening functions are by definition in their own society noncombatants. Women, children, and the aged were immune because they were unable to be soldiers; magistrates, some clergy, and teachers were exempted because of their useful function in society. Since such persons existed in every nation, furthermore, it was in the mutual self-interest of nations at war to observe certain limits with regard to them.[46]

Vattel included peasants who worked the land in his list of exceptions, a development in the customary law of nations, because of their utility to their own society and to occupying armies. It was "a laudable custom, truly worthy of those who value themselves on their humanity, and advantageous even to the enemy who acts with such moderation. By protecting the unarmed inhabitants, keeping the soldiery under strict discipline and preserving the country, a general procures an easy subsistence for his army, and avoids many evils and dangers." Characteristically, Vattel combined the dictates of self-interest and regard for duty to mankind in arguing that noncombatants be made exempt from harm. In an age where the occupation of strategic towns and territories constituted the primary tasks of the

46. Johnson, *Ideology, Reason, and the Limitation of War*, 247; Vattel, Book III, Chap. 5, secs. 69–70.

armed forces and where the large armies depended on the local populace for their needs, such arguments would be especially effective. Vattel no doubt would have taken comfort in John Wolf's remark that the French destruction of the Rhineland "aroused all Germany as Germany had not been moved in all its previous history."[47]

Having defined these limits in the conduct of war, Vattel moved on to consider what the state of war did permit. We have a right to deprive our enemy of his possessions and of everything which enables him to augment his strength. This is done with a view to bringing the enemy to reason and as compensation for the injustice one has presumably suffered. Although Vattel stated that "he who is engaged in war, derives all his right from the justice of his cause" so that "whoever takes up arms without lawful cause, can have absolutely no right whatever" and is "chargeable with all the evils, all the horrors of the war," the doctrine of the voluntary law of nations, as suggested above, requires that states adopt an act-as-if-he-is-just attitude. "Every acquisition, therefore, that has been made in regular warfare, is valid according to the voluntary law of nations, independently of the justice of the cause." There are movable and immovable possessions: a conqueror may take movable goods, but he cannot annex immovable possessions (territory and towns) until title is formally granted in a peace treaty.[48]

Questions about these stipulations occurred in Americans' debates about foreign policy. One of Madison's first references to Vattel occurred in connection with the question of whether slaves constituted movable or immovable property. Hamilton argued that the French annexation of Belgium during the French Revolutionary War constituted unjust conduct on the part of the French.[49] The Americans also turned to Vattel on many of the other issues of American foreign policy in the 1780s and 1790s: navigation rights, fulfilling treaty obliga-

47. Vattel, Book III, Chap. 8, sec. 147; Wolf, *Toward a European Balance of Power*, 104.
48. Vattel, Book III, Chap. 9, sec. 161–63; Chap. 11, secs. 183–84; and Chap. 13, sec. 195.
49. "Notes on Debates, Dec. 23, 1782," in William T. Hutchinson *et al.* (eds.), *The Papers of James Madison* (12 vols.; Chicago, 1962–   ), V, 437; "Pacificus, No. 2," in Syrett and Cooke (eds.), *Hamilton Papers*, XV, 55–63.

tions, sequestration of British debts, free passage, and compensation for slaves taken or lured away by the British during the American Revolution. It was, however, the issue of neutrality and the status of the alliance with France which would prove the most troublesome questions in the 1790s. These issues and questions are taken up in the next three chapters.

CHAPTER III

The American Situation
in the 1780s and 1790s

In the decades following the Declaration of Independence in 1776, the United States found itself involved in several wars and presented with the possibility of others, even after the long struggle with Britain over independence was resolved with the Treaty of Paris in 1783. Leading Americans recognized that the mere fact of having neighbors—Britain to the north and northwest, Spain to the south and southeast, Indian tribes scattered around the borders—and an active worldwide commerce provided the conditions which could lead to war. Alexander Hamilton in *Federalist* Number 6 declared that "it has . . . become a sort of axiom in politics that vicinity, or nearness of situation, constitutes nations natural enemies." Thomas Jefferson, in his *Notes on Virginia*, remarked that since Americans had attached themselves to seaborne commerce "wars must then sometimes be our lot." This understanding of the structural possibility of war required that some preparations for war be made, but it did not provide for knowing when and why war should be made or avoided and how it should be conducted. That knowledge involved using some process of political and moral reasoning to assess conflicting interests and obligations and to weigh the costs and benefits of pursuing a particular course of action at a particular time. While Americans preferred peace on moral and political grounds, they actively considered the resort to force on some specific issues, carefully defined with references to the law of nations.[1]

1. Vagts and Vagts, "The Balance of Power in International Law," 555.

67

The European Balance and the American Revolutionary War

The external setting in which American diplomacy under the new Constitution would have to work can best be approached by reviewing the international situation at the formal conclusion of the War of the American Revolution in 1783. In that war Britain had faced not only an uprising in its American colonies south of the Great Lakes but also threats to its position and power from European rivals. Where the Franco-Austrian rivalry (the House of Hapsburg vs. the House of Bourbon) had dominated the European system in the seventeenth century, the Anglo-French rivalry had come to dominate in the eighteenth century. The French and the Spanish, allies by the Bourbon "Family Compact," had both turned from policies which sought continental domination to ones which sought to reduce British naval strength and colonial holdings on which Britain's strong position in Europe depended.[2] The French had lost their North American possessions to the British in the disastrous Seven Years' War and had subsequently embarked on a vigorous program of rebuilding their navy for just such an effort to strike back at the British. By May 1778, at the time of the break with Britain, France and Spain had a combined strength of ninety ships of the line against seventy-two for Britain. American independence, as the British pamphleteer Arthur Young realized, was "the interest of all those powers in Europe, whom Britain rivals either in general power, naval dominion, trade, commerce, or manufactures."[3]

The Americans held out to the French the opportunity to make gains in the West Indies, sever the important American colonies from the British, and obtain access to American products and markets. As Madison would say several years later, the French had not entered the war simply to help the Americans achieve independence, but for "the commerce and gratitude of America" as well. Initially the Conti-

2. Ludwig Dehio, *The Precarious Balance*, trans. Charles Fullman (New York, 1962), 120–23.
3. Quoted in Richard W. Van Alstyne, *Empire and Independence: The International History of the American Revolution* (New York, 1965), 45.

68

nental Congress had hoped that British troubles in Europe combined with American resistance and the loss of American commerce would be sufficient to bring about independence. It soon became clear, however, that a more formal connection with Britain's rivals would be necessary. Even then, American leaders wanted to keep the connection strictly limited; as John Adams wrote a friend, "I am not for soliciting any political connection, or military assistance, or indeed naval, from France. I wish for nothing but commerce, a mere marine treaty with them."[4]

In February 1778 the United States and France signed a "Treaty of Amity and Commerce," constituting the first official recognition of the United States by a major power, each granting the other most-favored-nation status and other liberal trading privileges. The Americans found, though, that they had to take up political questions as well. A second "Treaty of Alliance" provided that if war should break out between France and Great Britain—almost certain to follow from the first treaty—France and the United States would fight together in a defensive alliance until American independence was assured. Neither party was to conclude a peace with Great Britain without the formal consent of the other; France guaranteed American independence and territory "forever" and renounced possession of any portion of the North American mainland lost to the British in 1763. In return the United States pledged to guarantee French possessions in the West Indies and not to oppose French conquests there. The French clearly had no intention of leaving the Western Hemisphere altogether. Within several months of the signing of the treaty, the French dispatched a fleet to aid the Americans, declared war with Britain, and entered into a series of naval battles with the British fleet.[5]

The United States also looked to the possibility of a treaty with Spain and dispatched John Jay to Madrid for that purpose in late

---

4. Adams is quoted by Felix Gilbert in his *The Beginnings of American Foreign Policy: To the Farewell Address* (New York, 1965), 47–48; Madison's views are presented in "Notes on Debates," in Hutchinson *et al.* (eds.), *Madison Papers*, VI, 441.

5. Alexander DeConde, *Entangling Alliance: Politics and Diplomacy Under George Washington* (Durham, N.C., 1958), 5.

1779. For their part, the Spanish saw in Britain's troubles with its colonies an opportunity to regain Gibraltar and Minorca and by reclaiming the Floridas and both banks of the Mississippi to secure the Gulf of Mexico and Spain's American colonies. These security considerations, supported by Spain's long-standing claims to rightful ownership of the New World based on a papal dispensation, also made the Spanish reluctant to provide any assistance to the Americans, who were already spreading into the Ohio and Mississippi valleys and who were demanding free navigation on the Mississippi River. When Spain did enter the war against Britain in 1779 it did so on the basis of an alliance with France and only on the understanding that Gibraltar would have to be taken before the war would cease. The Spanish continued to refuse to see Jay, recognize American independence, or grant the right of navigation which the Americans demanded; their only contribution to the American cause came from forcing the British to contemplate a multifront war, thereby keeping the British from bringing all their forces to bear in the American theater.

The other European states, led by Catherine of Russia and the seafaring neutrals, had formed a League of Armed Neutrality in 1780 and proclaimed a code of maritime principles for the protection of neutral shipping which struck at British commercial and maritime practice. Congress also quickly adopted its principles and tried to gain admittance, but the League did not invite the United States to join and its members pointedly refused to recognize the American government. Holland's adherence to the League and its refusal to honor its alliance with Britain brought Holland into the war against Britain in December 1780. Though Dutch shipping had indirectly helped the Americans, the Dutch also proved unwilling to recognize American independence until April 1782. Nevertheless, the League had the effect of isolating Britain from possible allies on the Continent. Thus for a brief and rare moment the continental powers had made common cause against Britain and, without intending to do so, contributed significantly to the establishment of American independence. The memory of this successful manipulation of the European balance system to force concessions from Britain would, however, remain the basis on which Jeffersonian strategic thinking rested for the next three decades.[6]

The British understood very well the vital role played by the American colonies in the imperial economy, whereby Americans provided essential raw materials in exchange for goods manufactured in Britain. Reflection on this system led some Britons and many Americans to think that if the Americans removed themselves from the British navigation system, England would be injured so severely that Parliament would gladly accede to American demands. England, already heavily in debt, would be brought to the edge of bankruptcy; the West Indies would face ruin; and the Irish textile industry, which depended on American materials, would be idled, leaving thousands unemployed and restive. Though American withdrawal did cause economic dislocation and financial hardship, commercial warfare proved to be insufficient, making the French alliance necessary. The British did try several times during the war to conciliate the Americans in order to regain something of the old relationship and to pull the United States away from the French orbit. They finally decided, in light of the forces arrayed against them, to grant independence and to work at restoring many of the privileges of the old imperial order. Indeed, the American peace commissioners held out to the British the prospect of complete reciprocity between the United States and England in trade and navigation as an inducement to come to terms. According to A. L. Burt, the preliminary draft treaty provided for the free navigation of the Mississippi, mutual free navigation of other British and American waters, and free trade between the United States and the British Empire.[7]

On the other hand, the war had not gone well for France, Spain, or Holland, despite British difficulties in the United States. The Spanish had retaken the Floridas and the Mississippi and the British had been defeated at Yorktown, but in the West Indies Britain had

6. Alexander DeConde, *A History of American Foreign Policy* (2d ed.; New York, 1971), 27–31.
7. A. L. Burt, *The United States, Great Britain, and British North America* (New Haven, 1940), 30; Paul Varg, *Foreign Policies of the Founding Fathers* (Baltimore, 1970), 2–75, provides useful background material.

strengthened her position, the Spanish could not take Gibraltar, a joint French and Spanish invasion of Britain had collapsed, and the Dutch had lost great amounts of shipping and commerce to British warships. Such evidence of British strength and the prospect of a potentially powerful new nation in North America led the French to consider peace with Britain. Unable to take Gibraltar, the Spanish demanded that France at least secure the Spanish possessions in the Americas by checking her American ally. Thus the French found themselves caught between the conflicting demands of their allies for land in the trans-Allegheny West and for navigation rights on the Mississippi. Moreover it seemed to some Americans that the French wanted to limit the size and strength of the new republic whose independence they were pledged to support. In effect the Americans were resisting the efforts of the French to establish a balance of power system on the North American continent, consisting of British, Spanish, and French colonies on the mainland and in the Caribbean, the new American republic, and an Indian state between the Ohio and the Mississippi; this vision, which France, Spain, and Britain all considered at one time or another, conflicted with the vision of continental empire which many Americans had.

In America French representatives refused to support plans to invade Canada (actually "British North America") or besiege Canadian cities. One of them told Congress in January 1779 that from the French point of view the United States had no claim to the Northwest Territories, that such ambitions went contrary to French relations with Spain, and that the United States was a commercial republic of thirteen states which would fall if it sought an inland empire. In 1782, under the influence of the French ambassador La Luzerne, Congress and Secretary for Foreign Affairs Robert Livingston offered to accept as a last resort in the peace negotiations a buffer native state in the western territories which would enjoy its independence under the guaranty of France, Spain, Great Britain, and America, and be open to the trade of those whose lands border on it. Such an arrangement would undoubtedly have helped allay Spanish fears about American expansion and in fact remained a persistent theme in Spanish diplomacy in the coming decades. It would have also made the United States more dependent on its French ally.[8]

In Paris, however, John Jay and John Adams smelled a plot to rob the country of its hinterland, which induced them to carry on separate peace negotiations with Great Britain. Though this ran counter to the spirit, if not the letter, of the alliance with France, the French acceded to it. Thus, before the definitive treaty was signed, when the United States informed France of the peace terms, France gave its formal consent though not without expressing shock about the Americans' conduct and about the generosity of the English in making peace. Still, there was a larger European settlement to be worked out, of which American independence was only a part. Moreover the American action solved for France the embarrassing dilemma it faced with respect to Spanish desires.

The Treaty of Peace

The 1783 Treaty of Paris, like most peace treaties, settled some issues, left others ambiguous, and created some new ones which would provoke fresh hostilities. The British, as part of their effort to conciliate the United States and perhaps weaken the American-French alliance, granted the United States generous terms which went far beyond what had been won on the battlefield. Not only was the United States granted independence; it also obtained the right to fish off of Newfoundland in the Grand Bank and the "liberty" to fish in other areas. The British also ceded the trans-Allegheny western lands south of the Great Lakes to the thirty-first parallel with the right to participate on equal terms in the navigation of the Mississippi. (It was assumed at the time that the Mississippi extended up into present-day Canada.) This grant conflicted with an earlier one included in a secret agreement between Spain and Great Britain which held the Americans far to the north of the thirty-first parallel. The Spanish preferred to hold to these earlier boundaries and contended that they

---

8. Van Alstyne, *Empire and Independence*, 217; Burt, *The United States, Great Britain, and British North America*, 27; Theodore Roosevelt, *Gouverneur Morris* (Boston, 1898), 105, states explicitly that France sought to establish a balance of power system in North America.

were not bound by the terms of the Anglo-American treaty. This meant that both the United States and Spain claimed an extensive tract of land in the Old Southwest, covering parts of Georgia, Tennessee, and Kentucky, and most of Alabama and Mississippi. Intentionally or not, the British had ensured continued conflict between the United States and Spain on the issue of territories and boundaries.[9]

The treaty further stipulated provisions which proved difficult or inconvenient for the signatories to comply with. The British had agreed that their forces would be withdrawn from United States territory "with all convenient speed" though no precise schedule was laid out, but when the Washington administration came into office six years later, the British still had not relinquished the forts they held on the Great Lakes. These posts assured control of the St. Lawrence Valley and the lucrative fur trade there. Each fort was near the border, but was strategically located to ensure continued dominance of the region and to provide security for Indian tribes friendly to the British. Americans naturally resented this affront to their sovereignty and had tried on various occasions to persuade the British to leave by appealing to the obligation to fulfill treaty commitments, but without success.

The British had also agreed not to carry away any public or private property, including slaves. During the war the British had gathered up slaves for work, to deprive their owners of their labor, and had promised the slaves freedom. Some had died while in British hands, but others were freed when the British left, and the southern slaveholders demanded their return or compensation for the loss of property. Northern antipathy to slavery abetted British noncompliance on this point, though American leaders protested from time to time. This had more to do with its diplomatic effect than with real desire to reenslave freed blacks. Alexander Hamilton, for example, argued that the evil of surrendering persons to slavery outweighed the good of restoring property to its rightful owners. Significantly this put Ham-

9. Van Alstyne, *Empire and Independence*, 220; Arthur Whitaker, *The Spanish-American Frontier, 1783–1795* (Boston, 1927), remains as the standard account of Spanish-American relations during this period.

ilton at odds with Vattel and caused him to argue against Vattel by appealing to the necessary law of nations. It is this willingness on Hamilton's part to appeal directly to the law of nature which distinguishes Hamilton from the English statesman Edmund Burke, with whom he is sometimes compared.[10]

For its part, the United States agreed that there was to be no "lawful impediment" to the collection of prewar debts by the British; that there would be no further persecution of Loyalists; and that Congress would "earnestly recommend" restitution of Loyalist or British property seized during the war. These agreements depended heavily on the persuasive power of the Continental Congress with the various state legislatures since the Congress lacked the legal authority to enforce compliance. The state governments rejected these efforts, and continued to exact a price from Loyalists for opposing the Revolution. For men like Hamilton the inability of Congress to fulfill its treaty obligations was embarrassing and troubling, although, as Jefferson pointed out, the Congress had done what it had pledged to do, namely to request legislation in accordance with the peace treaty. Still, the situation provided one argument for the creation of a strong central government. It also made the British bolder about imposing commercial restrictions on American shipping.[11]

The British and American negotiators had expected to complete a commercial treaty based on principles of free trade and navigation following ratification of the peace treaty, but several factors prevented its completion. When the British parliament saw how generous the British cabinet had been in its arrangements with the Americans, it adopted by a narrow margin a vote of censure of the government for the peace it had concluded. The purpose of the vote, according to A. L. Burt, was to upset Lord Shelburne but not the treaty. When Shelburne resigned, his successor William Pitt offered a bill of commercial reciprocity along the lines contemplated by Shelburne and

10. "Cabinet Opinion, July 9–11, 1795," in Syrett and Cooke (eds.), *Hamilton Papers*, XVIII, 415; "The Defense, No. 3," *ibid.*, XVIII, 5–9. One who compares Hamilton with Burke is Allan Hamilton, *The Intimate Life of Alexander Hamilton* (New York, 1910), 121.
11. Gilbert Lycan, *Alexander Hamilton and American Foreign Policy* (Norman, Okla., 1970), 63.

Parliament rejected it. The bill seemed to give away too much in return for uncertain benefits.

The writings and speeches of Lord Sheffield especially seemed to harden British hearts. Sheffield argued that the British economy was much stronger than most people believed; the copious data he had collected and published demonstrated that the British economy was dominant and could retain American trade within its orbit without making any concessions at all. Whereas Benjamin Franklin had argued that England needed America more than America needed England, Sheffield argued just the reverse. Americans would have to come to the British for capital and for manufactured goods which other European nations could not provide; moreover, British markets remained the best ones for American produce, but even here other sources of supply (British North America and the West Indies) kept Britain from too great a dependency on American raw materials. Thus, Britain should restore its navigation acts; there was no need to court the Americans to win back their trade since it would tend to come to Britain anyway, given British commercial policy. The weakness of the American government also contributed to the loss of a commercial treaty. Since the authority to regulate commerce lay with the individual states, the United States Congress could not act or effectively resist British commercial policy; competition between states for trade made it much easier for the British to set down strict navigation acts.

Instead of completing a commercial treaty, the British crown laid down orders-in-council which restored the navigation acts and applied them to American trade. These orders closed the West Indies to American ships and excluded American salt, meat, and fish from the islands. Trade with British North America was closely regulated; American lumber and wheat could be sent to the islands only if transported in British ships; and American fish, oil, and whale products were prohibited from British markets. That other American goods were allowed into Britain duty free seemed less significant to Americans accustomed to freer trade with Britain than the obstructions which Britain had created. Britain added to this policy of aloofness by refusing to exchange ambassadors with the new nation, later pointing to the inability of the United States government to fulfill its

76

treaty obligations as an excuse for this. In short, the hope of recon-
ciliation between the United States and Great Britain which attended
the peace negotiations soon gave way to resentment and mistrust,
while Americans kept pushing for the liberal trading order which had
seemed imminent with peace in 1783.[12]

Relations with France

The treaty with France remained more or less intact, although it
showed signs of strain because of French ties with Spain and because
of American suspicions about French intentions. Indeed, unbe-
knownst to the Americans, the French continued to entertain hopes
of regaining Louisiana from Spain. Efforts continued in both the
United States and France to expand commercial ties. The commercial
treaty liberalized trade between the two countries and granted American ships a limited right to trade with certain ports in the French
West Indies. In this manner France hoped to develop a thriving commerce, not merely between the American states and French colonies,
but between the United States and France itself.[13] The American ambassador to France, Thomas Jefferson, worked hard to break down
trade barriers: "In truth," he wrote the French secretary of foreign affairs, "no two countries are better calculated for the exchanges
of commerce. France wants rice, tobacco, potash, furs, and ship-
timber. We want wines, brandies, oils, and manufactures." Nevertheless, by 1789 there were clear signs that Americans preferred British
goods, and French merchants were objecting to the liberties granted
American commerce. Americans were also tied to France by the debt
owed France in payment for the many loans extended during the war.
In 1790 the United States owed almost twelve million dollars to
France, the Netherlands, and Spain. The Congress of the Confedera-

12. Burt, *The United States, Great Britain, and British North America*, 55–59; see
also William K. Woolery, *The Relation of Thomas Jefferson to American Foreign Policy*
(Baltimore, 1927).
13. Frederick Jackson Turner, "The Policy of France Toward the Mississippi Valley
in the Period of Washington and Adams," *American Historical Review*, X (January,
1905), 249–79; DeConde, *Entangling Alliance*, 20–26 and 449; and Oliver
Wolcott to Hamilton, July 10, 1795, in Syrett and Cooke (eds.), *Hamilton Papers*,
XVIII, 457.

tion proved unable to pay installments on the principal or even to keep up the interest payments, and France as the main creditor suffered the most. Though unable to collect on these debts, France was not entirely displeased with the situation; Alexander DeConde suggests that the French realized that a politically weak and financially unstable government would be more amenable to French control.[14]

The Franco-American alliance persisted also on the basis of a warm bond which existed between Americans and the people of France. Having fought in a common struggle and won independence with French assistance, Americans remained "in general extremely well affected to France," George Washington observed. During the American Revolution, Benjamin Franklin had captivated the French with demonstrations of his republican simplicity and sagacity so that when he returned to the United States in 1784 he left behind him an enduring legacy of goodwill among the French. Thomas Jefferson, his successor, acted in accordance with his belief that in regard to France "nothing should be spared, on our part, to attach this country to us. It is the only one on which we can rely for support, under every event. Its inhabitants love us more, I think, than they do any other nation on earth."[15]

Relations with Spain

America's relationship with the third major power with interests in the Western Hemisphere, Spain, remained consistently and unambiguously cool. Efforts to draw up a treaty during the war bore no fruit and no Spanish-American treaty was included in the general Treaty of Paris. The Americans insisted on free navigation of the Mississippi, which they had enjoyed since 1763 until the Spanish closed off the river in 1784. For the Americans free navigation was a *sine qua non*, being a natural, positive, and customary right. In a letter of

14. Jefferson to Vergennes, August 15, 1787, in Boyd *et al.* (eds.), *Jefferson Papers*, VIII, 389; Dumas Malone, *Jefferson and the Rights of Man* (Boston, 1951), 394–99; Lycan, *Alexander Hamilton and American Foreign Policy*, 106; and DeConde, *Entangling Alliance*, 17.
15. Jefferson to Madison, January 30, 1787, in Boyd *et al.* (eds.), *Jefferson Papers*, XI, 96.

instructions which James Madison, as chairman of the Foreign Affairs Committee in the Continental Congress, had written in 1780 to Jay in Spain, all three of these bases were explained. A citation to Vattel on the right of innocent passage on land when nations are at peace was extended to innocent use of the Mississippi as well. In addition, Madison argued, the Treaty of Paris of 1763 had made the Mississippi part of the British Empire, which meant that use of the river extended to the Americans and became the basis for the customary right which the Americans also claimed. Finally there was a characteristically American appeal to Spain's "commercial sagacity" in the increased trade which Spain would undoubtedly enjoy if the Mississippi were kept open to American trade.[16] The Spanish reasoned that admitting free navigation would only encourage American settlements in the trans-Appalachian West which would increase American pressures on bordering Spanish land. The British exacerbated these conflicts of interest when they apparently ceded parts of the Old Southwest to both parties. This had the effect of embroiling Spain and the United States in conflicting claims over territory until the ratification of the Adams-Onis Treaty in 1819.

Spain had tried several times since 1783 to make peace and offered in 1785 to make an alliance and a commercial treaty in return for renunciation of the free navigation claims. When Secretary for Foreign Affairs John Jay attempted to reach an understanding with the Spanish minister Gardoqui along those lines he found the southern states unalterably opposed to any concessions on the navigation claims. On the other hand, the seven commercial states in the Northeast voted for the exchange, revealing a deep sectional split. Since it took nine states to ratify a treaty under the Articles of Confederation, the Spanish offering came to naught. One reason southerners like James Madison opposed the proposed treaty was that they feared that Kentucky would secede if the United States conceded on their navigational claims. In fact, the Spanish were engaged in efforts to entice the secession of southwesterners and to create buffer Indian

16. "Draft of Letter to John Jay, Explaining His Instructions, October 17, 1780, in Hutchinson *et al.* (eds.), *Madison Papers,* II, 127–36.

states in the disputed territories. Rumors of these efforts no doubt contributed to American mistrust of Spanish intentions.[17]

With respect to the other European states, the United States sought only to nurture commercial ties. Favorable trade treaties were negotiated with the Netherlands, Sweden, Prussia, and Morocco between 1782 and 1787, but these had produced few tangible results. The expectation that the Europeans would leap at the chance to trade for American goods proved excessive, and by 1789 it was becoming increasingly clear that the Europeans were more deeply wedded to mercantile policies and Americans to British goods than many Americans had assumed.

The Constitution and the French Revolution

Against this background occurred two singular events which would have the most profound consequences for America's international relations: the establishment of the new Constitution and the initiation of the French Revolution. The former created a government "partly federal, partly national" empowered to declare war, regulate commerce, grant letters of marque and reprisal, and punish piracies and other offenses against international law; it also made treaties part of the law of the land. The weakness of the American government under the Articles of Confederation in the face of foreign threats and intrigue was a prominent theme in the discussions about the need to revise the basic charter of the United States. The first question which Publius, the pseudonymous author of the *Federalist Papers*, asked his readers to consider was "whether the people are not right in their opinion that a cordial Union, under an efficient national government, affords them the best security that can be devised against hostilities from abroad."[18]

Publius cited the inability of the United States to carry out or enforce treaty agreements as an additional weakness requiring the rem-

17. Worthington C. Ford, *The United States and Spain in 1790* (Brooklyn, N.Y., 1890), 11; also Jefferson to Archibald Stuart, January 25, 1787, in Boyd *et al.* (eds.), *Jefferson Papers*, IX, 218; and Jefferson to Madison, January 30, 1787, *ibid.*, XI, 96.
18. Hamilton, Jay, and Madison, *The Federalist Papers*, 42.

edy of a stronger national government. Alexander Hamilton, one of the men who wrote as "Publius," wrote with passion about the humiliation which the United States had experienced on this score: "There is scarcely anything that can wound the pride or degrade the character of an independent nation which we do not experience. Are there engagements to the performance of which we are held by every tie respectable among men? These are the subjects of constant and unblushing violation." Hamilton reviewed all the major foreign policy issues which confronted the United States and tried to show how much foreign policy failure stemmed from the weakness of the United States under the Articles. Nothing had been done about the foreign or the domestic debt; important territories and posts continued to be held against the rights and the interests of the United States, but the United States having neither "troops, nor treasury, nor government" could not even "remonstrate with dignity" much less repel the aggression; similarly the United States remained excluded from free navigation of the Mississippi although entitled to it by nature and by compact; the nation could do little to promote and protect its commerce; and public credit, indispensable in times of crisis, appeared to have been abandoned. "Is respectability in the eyes of foreign powers a safeguard against foreign encroachments?" asked Hamilton; and in reply he answered, "The imbecility of our government forbids them to treat with us." [19]

The Anti-Federalist opponents of the proposed constitution thought that this account exaggerated the weakness of the United States under the Confederation and the extent of the foreign threat, and that it proposed the wrong solution. Patrick Henry rightly detected in the Federalist arguments for respectability abroad dreams of national glory, wealth, and empire. Such dreams, if fulfilled, would undermine the essential quality of the American spirit: its love of liberty.

> Shall we imitate the example of those nations who have gone from a simple to a splendid Government? Are those nations more worthy of our imitation? What can make an adequate satisfaction to them for the loss they have suffered in attaining such a Government—for the loss of their

19. *Ibid.*, 106–107.

liberty? If we admit this Consolidated Government, it will be because we like a great splendid one. Some way or other we must be a great and mighty empire; we must have an army, and a navy, and a number of things; When the American spirit was in its youth, the language of America was different; Liberty, Sir, was then the primary object.[20]

Nevertheless, the Anti-Federalists admitted that some improvements in the Articles had to be made to mitigate interstate competition and potential anarchy and to strengthen the hand of American officials abroad in making commercial treaties. Jefferson, who shared several of the Anti-Federalist reservations about the proposed constitution, nevertheless agreed that the foreign debts had to be paid and commercial regulation authorized to give the country more weight in the eyes of European leaders. These admissions suggest why the Anti-Federalists had the weaker argument in the debate over the constitution and why in 1789 a government under the new constitution came into being. On the other hand we shall see that Anti-Federalist concerns about the domestic consequences of foreign policy for republican government and jealousy of the executive branch persisted as powerful themes in the partisan rhetoric of the 1790s.[21]

Those elected to office under the new constitution spent the first session of Congress simply organizing the government, filling its offices, and passing the necessary enabling legislation. The first Congress passed the Bill of Rights, created a federal judiciary, established the executive departments, debated the president's removal power, and passed a tariff law to raise revenue for the expenses of government. With these measures in place and with Congress adjourned, by early October of 1790 President Washington turned to foreign affairs.[22]

He gave attention first to British affairs and discussed with John Jay, Alexander Hamilton, and James Madison what to do about the western posts, British debts, and a commercial treaty. Jay and Hamilton urged Washington to act as soon as possible on these matters,

---

20. Cited in Storing, *What the Anti-Federalists Were For*, 31.
21. Jefferson to Edmund Randolph, August 3, 1787, in Boyd *et al.* (eds.), *Jefferson Papers*, XI, 672–73; Storing, *What the Anti-Federalists Were For*, 38–47 and 71–72.
22. Forrest McDonald, *The Presidency of George Washington* (New York, 1975), 32.

which had been pending for over five years, and Hamilton suggested that Gouverneur Morris, already in Europe, be asked to seek out the British ministry privately to sound out their intentions. Madison, who noted that Morris' imagination sometimes ran ahead of his judgment, suggested that if the discussions were not immediately necessary it would be better to wait for Jefferson, who was on his way back to Virginia from France. While Hamilton's reasons for pressing the matter have been questioned owing to his relationship with the British secret agent George Beckwith,[23] Washington seems to have been impressed with the need to renew contacts with the British as soon as possible. It would not be until 1795 and Jay's Treaty that these issues would be (at least temporarily) resolved. Washington's letter to Morris, however, expressed some optimism that the British would be more inclined to deal with the Americans now that a stronger government was in place. Sending Morris privately had the additional advantage of circumventing the problem that there had been no exchange of ambassadors and sending a minister to England without the assurance of reciprocation seemed unduly servile.

To Morris, Washington stressed that the new constitution put the United States in the position of being able to enforce its treaty commitments. When John Adams had attempted to negotiate a commercial treaty with the British between 1785 and 1788, he was told that one reason the British would not negotiate was that they did not believe the American government had the authority or power to enforce its will on the states and their citizens. That obstacle was now out of the way. Morris was to ask what the British intended to do about the western posts, the slaves which had been carried off, the need for a formal exchange of ministers, and the possibility of a treaty of commerce. Washington also observed that the Congress had considered, as a kind of threat, measures of commercial retaliation against British shipping, something he suspected that the British would be anxious to avoid.

Washington also turned his attention to Spanish affairs. Little had

---

23. DeConde, *Entangling Alliance*, 66–68; Lycan, *Alexander Hamilton and American Foreign Policy*, 102; Julian Boyd, *Number Seven* (Princeton, N.J., 1964).

occurred since the breakdown of the Jay-Gardoqui negotiations which had so incensed the southern delegates in Congress; Congress had postponed consideration of Spanish issues until after the formation of the new government, Gardoqui had returned to Spain, and a new monarch had been crowned in Spain. Washington wanted to make sure that the Spanish government realized that the United States could not yield on the point of free navigation, despite Jay's earlier apparent willingness to make concessions. It was a subject on which the Americans felt that they could afford to be insistent since right and time were on their side. The prodigious growth of American settlements in the West, the decline of Spanish power, and the failure of Spanish colonial policies all contributed to the American optimism.[24]

Finally, Washington continued to express optimism about the American relationship with France. To Frenchmen like Lafayette and the Comte de Moustier, Washington expressed his displeasure with continued American attachment to British goods and hoped that French commerce could replace British goods in American markets. In spite of French concessions and the efforts of American officials, however, most American trade ended up in British hands partly because of familiarity and habit, partly because of the British navigation laws, and partly because of the ready availability of British credit. Sooner or later the Washington administration and the Congress would have to address this fact and decide whether the United States ought to seek to alter the situation or to exploit it for other purposes. To alter the situation would mean to favor France by discriminating against British goods; to exploit it would mean to maintain or promote existing commercial patterns which favored the British. Washington eventually sided with his secretary of the treasury, Alexander Hamilton, who argued that the new nation's efforts to establish a respectable credit standing at home and abroad would fail without British trade. This meant loosening the Franco-American bonds and undermining the efforts of those like James Madison and Thomas Jefferson who sought to use French commerce as a counterweight to British monopoly. The Hamiltonian commitment to avoid

24. Washington to Morris, in John C. Fitzpatrick (ed.), *The Writings of George Washington* (39 vols.; Washington, D.C., 1931–44), XXX, 440–41.

antagonizing the British had to conflict at some point with the spirit, if not the letter, of the 1778 treaties.

The Franco-American alliance also underwent strains because of the French Revolution, the far-reaching consequences of which were only dimly perceived at the time. In the beginning Washington was cautiously optimistic about the events in France: he wrote Lafayette that "The revolution, which has taken place with you, is of such magnitude and of so momentous a nature that we hardly yet dare to form a conjecture about it. We however trust, and fervently pray that its consequences may prove happy to a nation, in whose fate we have so much cause to be interested."[25] Later, as the French Revolution evolved into an armed challenge to the European states system and to monarchical principles everywhere and as its conduct became increasingly brutal, Washington and others in the Federalist party turned against it. There remained many Americans, however, whose enthusiasm for the French cause stayed high, and this created special problems for an administration which saw itself as nonpartisan at home and neutral abroad. Partisanship for the French or for their British opponents quickly entwined itself into divisions already made evident by the disputes over the Hamiltonian system of finance. Thus the French Revolution contributed to a polarization in American political life which the activities of its ministers in America exacerbated.

The French Revolution created new strains in the fabric of international society as well. The attack on monarchical principles of legitimacy galvanized opposition to established authorities throughout Europe, setting "aristocrats" against "democrats." Its effects soon spilled over into the relations of states. Spain was the first to feel its effects, because the republican principles espoused by the French undermined the Bourbon Family Compact. This became clear during the Nootka Sound crisis of 1790. The crisis began with Spanish seizure of English merchant vessels on Vancouver Island and the claim to exclusive right to the west coast of North America. Britain rejected the claim and demanded compensation for the injury; when Spain refused and reasserted her claim, both sides began to mobilize for war. Spain asked France for support based on their alliance, but

25. Washington to Lafayette, *ibid.*, XXX, 448–49.

France balked; Spain consequently gave in to the British demands and the crisis passed. During the period of tension and uncertainty, Washington had asked his cabinet officers about the proper American response, since war between Britain and Spain, if it were to break out, would occur on the North American continent and perhaps on American soil. Secretary of State Jefferson in particular saw in the brewing trouble an opportunity to press Spain for concessions on the navigation and boundary questions in return for American neutrality and for a pledge to secure the west bank of the Mississippi for Spain. He also sought to use the good offices of the French, still allies to both, to persuade the Spanish to accede to American demands. Jefferson would return to this strategy later in his efforts as president to gain the Floridas from Spain, but the Spanish no longer trusted the French, and their relations deteriorated so much that by 1793 Spain had entered into an alliance with Great Britain against revolutionary France.[26]

These new developments would find the American negotiators in Madrid, William Short and William Carmichael, with instructions based on an understanding of alliance relationships quite the reverse of those which they found. Designed to take advantage of Spanish-English antagonism displayed in the Nootka Sound crisis, their instructions were irrelevant by late 1792. Instead there appeared a threat from the combined forces of Spain in Louisiana and Florida and Britain in British North America to American lands in the West, with French pretensions to Louisiana lurking in the background.

War in Europe and American Neutrality

As President Washington's second term of office began in the spring of 1793, he and his administration faced the problem of impending war in Europe as a result of the French Revolution. Austria and Prussia had already formed an alliance against France, Spain was moving against France, and it seemed more and more probable that Great Britain would be drawn into the contest as well. The Americans real-

26. DeConde, *History of American Foreign Policy*, 61; Alfred Bowman, "Jefferson, Hamilton, and American Foreign Policy," *Political Science Quarterly*, LXXI (March, 1956), 18–41, emphasizes Jefferson's realism in taking this position.

ized that war between France and Great Britain would have serious ramifications for American policy and commerce; in particular Great Britain with her powerful navy, her commercial dominance, and her position in British North America posed a grave potential threat to American security. One vital question for Washington to consider was how to address that threat best.

Some, like Secretary of the Treasury Hamilton, believed that it was imperative for the United States to avoid giving unnecessary offense to Britain, especially in light of manifold American weaknesses. Thus, in conversation with the British envoy George Hammond, Hamilton in March declared his intention to incline the United States to "as strict a neutrality as may not be directly contrary to its engagements." Others, like Secretary of State Jefferson and his fellow Virginian, Representative James Madison, believed that the United States ought to maintain its ties with France to counter British power and to moderate British conduct. They also noted the desirability of remaining at peace with the warring parties and urged a policy of "fair neutrality," but one which did not renounce American ties with France of the 1778 treaties of alliance and commerce. Moreover, they thought that Hamilton overestimated the British position and underestimated the American.[27]

When word reached the United States in April that war had indeed broken out between France and Great Britain, Holland, Spain, and Portugal, Washington with the advice and consent of his cabinet issued a proclamation designed to prevent American citizens from participating on one side or the other; without such a statement disavowing the actions of enterprising or enthusiastic citizens, the country might find itself drawn into a conflict it wanted to avoid.

The apparent unanimity of the cabinet behind the proclamation masked the deep disagreements within it about the meaning of impartiality, which in turn reflected differences about where "the duty and the interest," as the proclamation put it, of the United States lay. These differences had been clearly articulated as responses to a series of questions which the president had sent to the cabinet members the

27. "Conversations with George Hammond, March–April, 1793," in Syrett and Cooke (eds.), *Hamilton Papers*, XIV, 193; Jefferson to Madison, April 28, 1793, in Ford (ed.), *Jefferson Works*, I, 302.

day before they met in mid-April 1793 to discuss the proper course of action in light of the new European situation. The key issue raised in the list of questions concerned the status of the treaties of alliance and commerce with France. As the fourth question put it: "Are the United States obliged by good faith to consider the Treaties, heretofore made with France as applying to the present situation of the parties? May they either renounce them, or hold them suspended 'till the government of France shall be established?" If it was decided that the treaties remained in force, could they be maintained consistent with a policy of neutrality, and in what sense or under what conditions would the American guaranty of the French West Indies still apply? Finally, what should the United States do about the new French envoy to America, Edmund Genêt, who was expected soon and who might call on the United States to live up to its treaty obligations with France? [28]

During the cabinet meeting Hamilton, in arguing that the turmoil in France and in Europe gave the United States grounds to suspend the treaties, appealed to the authority of Vattel. Jefferson was not swayed by the citation, but it did cause Edmund Randolph, the attorney general, to reconsider his opposition to Hamilton's proposal. Unfortunately a copy of Vattel's work was not available at the moment and the meeting soon adjourned, in part so that the law-of-nations authorities could be consulted. Jefferson wrote to Madison, "Would you suppose it possible that it would have been seriously proposed to declare our treaties with France void on the authority of an ill-understood scrap in Vattel . . . and that it should be necessary to discuss it?" Thus provoked, he spent a week preparing a written opinion for the president on the subject of the proper interpretation of the law of nations about the questions raised by Hamilton. Grotius, Wolff, Pufendorf, and Vattel all came under his scrutiny. [29]

The different appraisals and recommendations offered by Hamilton and Jefferson foreshadowed the bitter partisanship which attended the ratification of Jay's Treaty two years later. Indeed, Jefferson

28. Washington's questions may be found in Syrett and Cooke (eds.), *Hamilton Papers*, XIV, 326.
29. Jefferson to Madison, April 28, 1793, in Ford (ed.), *Jefferson Works*, I, 301; "Opinion on the French Treaties," *ibid.*, I, 295.

saw that treaty and the subsequent quasi-war with France as the logical outcome of the Hamiltonian rationale for the neutrality proclamation. Arguments like his appeared in public soon after the proclamation was published. The arrival of Genêt and the pro-French feelings of many Americans, particularly in the South and West, assured public controversy on the matter. When Hamilton as "Pacificus" defended the administration, Jefferson wrote Madison, begging him to take up his pen against Hamilton, which Madison reluctantly did under the pseudonym "Helvidius." Although this debate between the principal collaborators of *Federalist Papers* is most often treated as a debate about the nature of executive power in a constitutional order, it originated as a debate about foreign policy.

Both sides, in presenting their cases to President Washington (who decided, against Hamilton, not to suspend the treaties) and then to the general public, appealed to the body of the modern science of international politics and law. According to Aristotle, rhetoric or the art of persuasion concerns itself with probabilities and with propositions "generally admitted" to be true "for scientific discourse is concerned with instruction [*i.e.*, logical proof] . . . but our proofs and arguments as rhetoricians must rest on generally accepted principles."[30] Even the rhetoric of statesmanship which seeks to lead public opinion must begin with what that public believes to be true. An examination of the arguments put forward offers instructive insights into the hold which the modern understanding of the law of nations had on the American mind which allowed or perhaps required the appeal to duty and to interest made in the proclamation. Those arguments and that understanding are the general focus of the following chapters.

The French declaration of war against Britain on February 1, 1793, created a host of new problems for the United States. Tied by treaty to France, but by Hamilton's financial system to Britain, split in sentiment between Federalists and Republicans (or, pejoratively, as Anglomen and Gallomen), and by its weakness unable to enforce its claims against the major powers, the United States government sought to make its way through a difficult passage. Neutrality would

30. Aristotle, *Rhetoric*, I, 1.

prove difficult to maintain as both France and Britain chose to seize American ships and goods rather than let them fall into the hands of their adversary. These depredations of American commerce, when combined with grievances over the western posts, the failure to provide compensation for the freed slaves, and British commercial practice, brought the United States and Great Britain to the brink of war between 1793 and 1795. This was finally averted by the negotiation and ratification of Jay's Treaty which removed some of the issues which had soured the Anglo-American relationship. On the other hand the success of Jay's efforts meant a growth in antagonism with the French, who claimed that the treaty violated the 1778 accords (though the Jeffersonians were perhaps even more vehement on this point than the French). Thus the wars of the French Revolution and the subsequent Napoleonic Wars, which pitted the French against the English and which lasted more or less uninterruptedly until the Congress of Vienna in 1815, created painful choices for the leaders of the United States.

Throughout this period Americans framed their problems about the rights of neutrality in much the way that they had addressed earlier objects of their foreign policy. Certainly their discussions of actual and potential resorts to force show that foreign policy was not justified as increasing American power as such, but was defined by specific issues and couched in the language of the law of nations: fulfilling treaty obligations, achieving free navigation on the Mississippi, removing impediments to trade, resisting impressment, and securing neutrality. This reliance on the law of nations did not preclude considerations of power, and in fact the major figures of American diplomacy understood that it was only through the workings of the European balance of power system that the United States could achieve its objectives. However, this understanding did not preclude great differences of view about how this could be done.

CHAPTER IV

The Hamiltonian Approach

One American response to the world crisis brought on by the French Revolution and the outbreak of war in Europe was the Federalist or Hamiltonian response. Although Hamilton served as secretary of the treasury, he played a major role in the formulation of American foreign policy during the 1790s. This exertion of influence in an area nominally in the jurisdiction of the secretary of state would itself have caused friction between cabinet officers, but the personal antagonism Hamilton and Jefferson—and their followers—came to feel had substantive roots as well. Agreement that the American national interest must be served did not necessitate agreement on what that interest was or how to achieve it. Such divergence of opinions extended to the use of the European balance and to the use of the law of nations.

Hamilton's views on these subjects emerge in an examination of four cases or episodes: the Nootka Sound crisis of 1790, the controversy over the French treaties in 1793, the defense of the Jay Treaty in 1795, and the endorsement of the quasi war with France in 1798/99. In private letters, in cabinet opinions, and especially in pseudonymous public articles, Hamilton laid out the Federalist approach in each of these matters. At various times John Quincy Adams, Fisher Ames, Rufus King, and other Federalists took up their pens to join the public debate, but Hamilton's efforts and his work as "Pacificus," "Americanus," "Camillus," and "Titus Manlius" in "The Stand" remain as the best expression of Federalist views on foreign policy.

91

In each of these there are extensive references to the law of nations and many citations to the approved writers on the subject. These references are fewest in "The Stand," but there the controlling concern is the threat of universal empire from France, a threat which Vattel and the law of nations taught was just cause for war. These documents reveal a common structure, reflecting the way that Hamilton organized ideas. In each Hamilton first treated the issues of rights and the law of nations, then he offered a course of action for the United States to pursue in the particular circumstance, according to the means at its disposal. This order strongly resembles that established by Vattel where he speaks first of "justificatory rights," then of motives or "interests," and finally of prudence or proportionality as a means-ends calculation.

Two other features of Hamilton's approach ought to be noted at the outset. Hamilton decided very quickly that the course the French Republic had set for itself in 1792 and 1793 fundamentally threatened the European balance of power system. This judgment came sooner to Hamilton than to most of his contemporaries and to many historians.[1] Some Jeffersonians, however, would admit the threat only after the Treaty of Ghent had been signed in 1815. Hamilton's quickness to judge was no doubt affected by domestic considerations and the threat to his financial system which a French-oriented neutrality would have entailed,[2] but also inherent in Hamilton's judgment was his understanding of the balance of power system and the just-war theory laid out by Vattel.

The second feature of Hamilton's thought which ought to be noted is that he consistently called for the nation to arm and to negotiate simultaneously. Hamilton was very sensitive to the effects that arms could have in a dispute and also in negotiations as an indication, at the very least, of one's seriousness. If negotiations should fail, the nation would still be in a good position to press its claims through force, having armed itself in preparation for that contingency. It is wrong simply to charge Hamilton with seeking military

1. Gulick, *Europe's Classical Balance of Power*, 96–97; Howard, *War in European History*, 80–82.
2. Bowman, "Jefferson, Hamilton, and American Foreign Policy," 33; Joseph Charles, *The Origins of the American Party System* (New York, 1956), 3–36.

honor at the expense of his country, because he consistently advocated negotiations as the best way for the nation to address its adversaries. Nevertheless, he also concluded that at times war was indeed preferable to further negotiations, which was the position he reached during the administration of John Adams and the period of the quasi war with France.

Hamilton and American Neutrality

Neutrality had been the great desideratum of American foreign policy from the early days of the Revolution; even though necessity had compelled the Americans to draw up an alliance with France, American statesmen generally understood the best policy to be that of remaining as little entangled as possible in the policies and controversies of the European nations. Hamilton, in his cabinet paper on the Nootka Sound question, reiterated the point that the soundest policy for the United States was "to steer as clear as possible of all foreign connection, other than commercial, and in this respect to cultivate intercourse with all the world on the broadest basis of reciprocal privilege."[3] However, with the possibility of general war in Europe, the treaties with France could jeopardize the neutrality and freedom of action which Hamilton sought for the United States and it was this problem which the European crisis made an acute concern. The situation seemed to call for a suspension, at least, of the French treaties, but the problem was how to reconcile that with the general obligation to keep one's promises.

Hamilton saw the unsettled political situation in 1793 in France and in Europe as an opportunity to suspend the French treaties at least until a legitimate government had been established, though he confided to John Jay that he doubted that the United States "could *bona fide* dispute the ultimate obligation of the Treaties."[4] This was nevertheless the course he advocated in mid-April, when the cabinet took up the questions of how to receive Genêt and whether to issue a proclamation of neutrality. Later, his public defense would take a somewhat different approach, in line with Washington's thoughts on

3. "Nootka Sound Opinion," in Syrett and Cooke (eds.), *Hamilton Papers*, VII, 52.
4. Hamilton to John Jay, April 3, 1793, *ibid.*, XIV, 298.

the matter. His cabinet argument for suspension rested on three points: a) the nature of the treaties with France, b) the provisional nature of the French government, and c) the danger to the United States if the treaties were not suspended.

During the cabinet meeting Secretary of State Jefferson had objected on constitutional, legal, and prudential grounds. He doubted that the executive had the authority to suspend the treaties, considered Hamilton's interpretation of the law of nations tendentious, and argued that a price be put on American neutrality, with the hope that the belligerents would make concessions to gain American neutrality.[5] Jefferson also wanted the United States to remain neutral, but he was concerned about how that neutrality would be presented to the world; he did not want the United States to appear to be siding with monarchy. It was decided during the meeting to issue a proclamation forbidding American citizens to take sides in the hostilities, though the word neutrality was avoided in deference to Jefferson's scruples. In addition it was agreed to receive Genêt, but the question of how to receive him was left unresolved and the cabinet adjourned on that and the question of suspending the treaties in light of the authorities on the law of nations. Each member later submitted his opinion in writing to the president with Secretary of War Henry Knox content to follow Hamilton's lead.

Before we turn to Hamilton's public face as "Pacificus" and "Americanus" we ought to examine his private or cabinet view. Hamilton's approach in his written opinion followed the pattern of his Nootka Sound opinion. In 1790, with Britain and Spain on the brink of war, Washington had wanted to know what his principal officers would advise the United States to do if Great Britain requested permission to march across American territory from Detroit to Mississippi to confront the Spanish forces in Louisiana. Hamilton divided his answer into three sections: first, there was the question of the right of the United States to refuse or to grant the British request for passage in the light of the law of nations; second, what would be the consequences of exercising or not exercising those rights; and third, what

5. McDonald, *The Presidency of George Washington*, 126.

was the strategic view that the United States ought to have in making its decisions.

Refusing to grant the request could be grounded in the rights of sovereignty, but Britain would probably appeal to the principle of the right of free passage. Thus Hamilton had to consider the question: what is the status of the right of passage in the opinion of the authorities? He reviewed for the president the opinions of Pufendorf, Barbeyrac, Grotius, and finally Vattel, "perhaps the most accurate and approved of the writers on the law of nations," and concluded from them that "there exists in the practice of nations and the dogmas of political writers a certain vague pretension to a right of passage in particular cases, and according to circumstances, which is sufficient to afford to the strong a pretext for claiming and exercising it, when it suits their interests, and to render it always dangerous to the weak to refuse, and, sometimes not less so, to grant it."[6]

For a weak country like the United States against a much stronger one like Great Britain, in considering the consequences of refusing or consenting to a claimed right of passage, the point of prudence was to "make choice of that course which threatens the fewest or the least, or sometimes the least certain" of evils. While acceding to the British request would have its dangers, refusing would have even greater ones, not least of which would be the inability of the United States to sustain its refusal by force of arms. Finally, the long-term strategic interests of the United States required gaining navigation rights on the Mississippi and a port on its mouth which could be gained only at Spain's expense. By 1798 Hamilton would expand these interests to include the Floridas and the detachment of South America from Spain. Implicit in Hamilton's analysis was his presumption that the chief objects of American foreign policy could be gained only with some sort of cooperation with the British. This did not necessarily require a formal treaty with Britain but would be the sort of informal cooperation where British interests coincided with American interests. All of these considerations led him to the conclusion that the United States, if asked, should allow the British to pass

6. "Nootka Sound Opinion," in Syrett and Cooke (eds.), *Hamilton Papers*, VII, 41 and 47.

through United States territory. For Hamilton, the inability of the United States to enforce its sovereign rights against claims of the right of passage was a decisive consideration. Nevertheless, Hamilton also counseled that if the British did not ask, ignoring even the most minimal acknowledgments of American sovereignty, then the United States ought to take up arms against Britain. Here was just cause for war, and Hamilton considered it imperative that the United States defend itself in that case, however improbable the prospects of American success.[7]

Hamilton's cabinet paper on the French treaties, though not the tour de force the earlier opinion was, also began with the law of nations and then moved to consider the consequences of alternative actions in light of the nation's character and interests. First, he held that it was permissible by the law of nations for the United States to elect to suspend the treaties with France with the eventual right of renunciation. This was not based on a denial of the right of a nation to change its form of government but it followed from the very nature of the treaties with France. Drawing on a distinction found in most of the legal authorities, including Vattel, Hamilton insisted that the treaties with France were personal treaties and not real treaties. Personal treaties attached to the persons of the contracting parties and secured some private interest; real treaties, on the other hand, were fixed to the body of the state. Real treaties bound the nations which contracted together notwithstanding any changes that occurred in their form of government; personal treaties expired with the passing of the persons who made them. If the United States had made its agreement with Louis XVI, which Hamilton argued that it had, then the treaty was a personal treaty and with the king's death the treaty expired as well. Thus the obligation of the United States to France expired with the execution of the king. Perhaps no other distinction points to the fundamental difference between the absolutist eighteenth century and the democratic twentieth century as does this distinction. Nevertheless, some people in the twentieth century have made a comparable distinction in distinguishing executive agree-

---

7. *Ibid.*, VII, 47; Hamilton to McHenry, June 27, 1799, and Hamilton to Rufus King, January 21, 1799, *ibid.*, XXII, 425–27.

ments and treaties ratified in the constitutional way, a comparison which suggests the essential nature of the executive power.[8]

Hamilton regarded the government which had dispatched Genêt as ambassador as provisional in character (it described itself that way) and as one whose legitimacy was one of the disputed points in the war. It followed that Genêt ought to be received in a way which signaled only American acknowledgment of the provisional character of his government; such a reception would notify the world that the United States was withholding its judgment on the continuance of the treaties until a secure and generally accepted French government was established. Moreover, Hamilton maintained, formal recognition of Genêt would violate neutrality by showing that the United States was taking sides in the French civil war, thereby breaching the norm of nonintervention.

Hamilton also argued, with explicit citations to Vattel, that if a change of government rendered a treaty with another nation useless, dangerous, or hurtful to that other nation "it is plain dictate of reason, that the latter will have a right to renounce those treaties." If anything, the treaties with France in their character as personal treaties, *i.e.*, treaties with the king, would oblige the United States to take up arms to restore the monarchy. Citing Pufendorf, Hamilton closed this question by stating that alliances with kings are made against foreign, not internal enemies. This relieved the United States of any responsibility to intervene on behalf of the king against the revolutionary party in the civil war then occurring in France.

Hamilton's sometimes tortured reasoning on the French treaty reflected the problematic character of treaty commitments in a balance of power system. States that enter into treaty arrangements with others want some assurance that each party to the bargain will keep its promises. On the other hand, the balance system, which is a system of alliances, sometimes requires alliances to shift. In effect the requirements of the system mean that treaties of alliance must be considered less binding than other treaties. For this reason, it was often

8. Hamilton and Henry Knox to Washington, May 2, 1793, *ibid.*, XIV, 377 and 384; the distinction between real and personal treaties can be found in Vattel, Book II, Chap. 12, secs. 183–95; Louis Henkin, *Foreign Affairs and the Constitution* (New York, 1972), 176–87.

said that every treaty contained an implied clause, the *clausula rebus sic stantibus*, which provided that a treaty was binding only so long as "things stand as they are." How to prevent this doctrine from being used to excuse the breach of a treaty obligation merely because it is inconvenient has proved difficult; nevertheless, the doctrine was one effort to deal with the problem of changing circumstances and shifts in power.[9]

It followed from these considerations based on the law of nations that the United States had the right to hold the operation of the treaties suspended and it was left to Hamilton to show that suspension was consistent with the nation's character and with its interests. National character or honor suggested that the United States show respect for its former ally the king by not throwing its weight behind the new provisional government, while at the same time honoring the principles of the right of nations to change their governments by not supporting the king's successors. In addition the national character would be damaged by too close an association with the French revolutionaries, whose revolution had become seriously blemished. By its crimes and extravagances the French Revolution had soiled the once glorious and respectable struggle for liberty.[10]

The interests of the United States lay clearly in peace. By holding the treaties suspended, the United States would provide fewer grounds to antagonize France and Britain than if it did not, and it would more easily avoid a war from which it could expect few benefits. If the United States did not suspend the treaties, then it would have to notify France that the guaranty was inoperative since theirs was an offensive war and the treaties covered only defensive wars. This would certainly displease the French more than suspending the treaties, whichever of the parties in France finally prevailed. Or the United States could plead inability to help, which Hamilton regarded as a disgraceful excuse. With characteristic thoroughness Hamilton considered the consequences of suspension or not if the republican party won or if the monarchical party won, though he

9. J. L. Brierly, *The Law of Nations* (Oxford, 1963), 334–45.
10. Hamilton to Washington, May 2, 1793, in Syrett and Cooke (eds.), *Hamilton Papers*, XIV, 407.

seemed to think it more probable that the latter would be restored to power in view of the armies ranged against the French republicans.[11]

President Washington chose not to suspend the treaties, a choice made difficult by the quick recognition which the United States had extended the provisional government in France, but he did appear to accept Hamilton's views on the inapplicability of the French treaty. Hamilton had rejected this option, because he thought that asserting the inapplicability of the treaties would be more provocative than suspension. Nevertheless, it was this course of action which Hamilton had to defend when he took up his pen to meet the storm of criticism which, in spite of Washington's caution, met the proclamation and which questioned its constitutionality, morality, legality, and propriety.

As we shall see, Hamilton made a powerful public defense of the administration as "Pacificus" and as "Americanus." John Quincy Adams made his own contribution as "Marcellus" and as "Columbus" and it was this defense, which launched Adams' diplomatic career. While Hamilton and Adams sometimes emphasized different points (Adams used the Bible as an authority; Hamilton developed a much more thorough doctrine of executive power), they both endeavored to teach the public what the interest and duty of the United States was within the framework of the law of nations. Their work represented an effort to show the public the way of prudence within the context of a republican constitutional order and within an accepted pattern of behavior among civilized states.

The Argument of Pacificus

Hamilton began his defense of the neutrality proclamation by noting that objections to it had tended to endanger peace, weaken public confidence in the executive, and reduce the obstacles to the overturn of the recently adopted constitution. He assumed that his audience valued peace, Washington's leadership, and the Constitution and he sought to show that the president's policy tended to promote the gen-

---

11. "Pacificus, No. 1," *ibid.*, XV, 42; Henkin, *Foreign Affairs and the Constitution*, 39–50.

erally accepted goods of peace and constitutional order. It was not enough, of course, simply to identify Washington's policies with those goods; he would have to satisfy the "sensible and well-informed" part of the community; he had to meet and overcome the objections which gave reasonable men pause.

Hamilton first treated the objection that the proclamation was issued under improper authority by the executive. All admitted the right of government to conduct foreign policy, declare neutrality, and regulate citizen conduct in the relations between states. It was the executive within any government which was the natural organ of intercourse between nations; treaties were made and interpreted as a function of that power. Foreign affairs fell naturally in the province of the executive with a few clear exceptions. The American constitution reflected this commonsense understanding so that the president was well within his rights to interpret the treaty with France in such a way that it was not inconsistent with a Proclamation of Neutrality: "While therefore the legislature can alone declare war, can alone actually transfer the nation from a state of peace to a state of war—it belongs to the 'executive power' to do whatever else the laws of nations cooperating with the treaties of the country enjoin, in the intercourse of the United States with foreign powers."[12]

Hamilton next turned to the objection that the proclamation violated the treaty with France. Though he had argued privately on other grounds, Hamilton, relying on the authority of Vattel and Burlamaqui, stressed the distinction between offensive and defensive wars to insist that the treaties with France were defensive in nature and hence inapplicable in this situation. France's declaration of war and initiation of hostilities clearly made her the offensive party whatever the merits of her cause, and this made the treaty with France nonoperational. Central to Hamilton's reasoning was Vattel's distinction between legal or positive right—the voluntary law of nations—and moral right—the necessary law of nations. The word *duty* in the proclamation encompassed both of these but Hamilton separated them to strengthen his case. For the United States the only question would have to be who began the war; this followed from the duties

12. "Pacificus, No. 2," in Syrett and Cooke (eds.), *Hamilton Papers*, XV, 57–58.

of the United States under the voluntary law of nations: "When a war breaks out between two nations, all other nations, in regard to the positive rights of the parties and their positive duties toward them, are bound to consider it as equally just on both sides." For Hamilton to say that France was the offensive power in the war was different than for him to say that France was the unjust power (though Hamilton would suggest that too). He thus preserved the distinction between offensive and unjust wars which has been denied in the twentieth century, where all offensive wars are wars of aggression. The voluntary law of nations alone provided sufficient grounds for nonexecution of the treaty; since the French treaties were explicitly defensive, the United States had no obligation to fulfill them. Nevertheless, the necessary law of nations required that the justness of France's war also be considered.

The Just War and the Balance of Power

In arguing that France was the unjust power, Hamilton pointed to a) the French threat to the balance of power system, b) French violations of her treaty obligations, c) French declarations of opposition to monarchical principles, which made France an enemy to all monarchies and which violated the norm of noncriticism of the regimes of one's neighbors, and d) French violations of *jus in bello* constraints or what Michael Walzer terms "the war convention." Like the authorities on which he drew, Hamilton located the basis for the maintenance of the balance of power system within the law of nations. This made a threat to the system by one power seeking dominance punishable by the other nations in the name of the law of nations:

> There is no principle better supported by the doctrines of writers, the practice of nations, and the dictates of right reason, than this—that whenever a nation adopts maxims of conduct tending to the disturbance of the tranquility and established order of its neighbors, or manifesting a spirit of self-aggrandisement—it is lawful for other nations to combine against it, and, by force, to control the effects of those maxims and that spirit. The conduct of France, in instances which have been stated calmly and impartially viewed, was an offence against the law of nations, which naturally made it a common cause among them to check her career.[13]

13. Hamilton to Washington, May 2, 1793, *ibid.*, XIV, 407.

One indication of French intentions was the way it had disregarded its treaty obligations. By violating its treaty with Holland on navigation rights, by taking steps to reopen Antwerp, which the British had had closed by treaty, and by incorporating territories taken by arms rather than holding them as bargaining chips for a future peace, France had taken up arms against the law of nations. This renunciation by France of its formal treaty obligations could legitimately be regarded as just cause for war by those arrayed against France. Britain could plausibly claim that it was acting on the conviction that, as W. Allison Phillips has put it, "it was incumbent upon her to champion established rights, guaranteed by the public law of Europe, against a power for which neither established rights nor international law had any validity."[14] For Hamilton, French actions showed an intention to build a continental empire; French declarations about liberating all Europe made Hamilton doubly suspicious.

One of the most unsettling features of the French Revolution was its attack on the monarchical principles that sustained many of the European states. French statements that France would defend all the friends of republican principles seemed to re-create a Europe torn by religious strife where the principles of internal rule came under the scrutiny of other states. As suggested earlier, the doctrine of sovereign rights was developed in part to delegitimize such interference. As explicated by Vattel, the law of nations was the application of the law of nature to sovereign states; its focus was on external, not internal, liberty. In other words the rights of sovereignty required that other nations not intervene in the internal affairs of their neighbors. Hamilton charged that the French had violated this rule by encouraging the overthrow of monarchs everywhere: "The pretext of propagating liberty can make no difference. Every nation has a right to carve out its own happiness in its own way, and it is the height of presumption in another to attempt to fashion its political creed."[15]

For Hamilton the justice of the war on France's side was "not a

14. W. Allison Phillips and Arthur Reede, *Neutrality in the Napoleonic Era* (New York, 1936), 6. Vol. II of Phillips and Reede, *Neutrality: Its History, Economics, and Law*, 3 vols.

15. Hamilton to Washington, May 2, 1793, in Syrett and Cooke (eds.), *Hamilton Papers*, XIV, 407.

little problematical." This was true in spite of French claims that its cause was the cause of liberty. In the French Convention of 1792 Revolutionary France challenged all Europe in saying that she would grant fraternity and assistance to every people who should desire to recover its liberty. Hamilton called himself a friend of liberty, but not when that liberty was imposed by one nation on another, which amounted to nothing more than interferences by one nation in the internal affairs of another. Finally, the beheading of the king and his family and the summary arrest and execution of thousands of aristocrats and alleged enemies of the Revolution in the ongoing turmoil in France showed none of the restraint intended by the *jus in bello* constraints of proportionality and discrimination. These excesses provided one more reason why the French could hardly claim justice on their side.[16]

In finding France's case morally, as well as legally, questionable, Hamilton did not mean to enlist the United States on the side of Britian against France; he intended rather to show the ambiguity of the French claim to justice, thereby releasing the United States of any moral obligation. As for the moral obligation *against* France (politically impossible in any case) Hamilton remarked, "I have no where found it maintained that the justice of a war is a consideration which can oblige a nation to do what its formal obligations do not require." That was a consideration in the realm of imperfect rights and duties, where nations could elect to help others but were not formally required to do so.[17]

Having considered the legal and the moral case for France, Hamilton turned to the political or prudential case. The essential criteria here were the prospects of success and the weighing of potential advantages against potential "mischiefs and perils" for the United States. With most of Europe, particularly the maritime powers, ranged against France, and with the United States "wholly destitute of naval force" it was unlikely that the United States could offer much mate-

16. Hamilton to Lafayette, April 28, 1798, *ibid.*, XXI, 450; McDonald, *The Presidency of George Washington*, 118–19.
17. "Americanus, No. 1," *ibid.*, XV, 570–72; Hamilton to Lafayette, April 28, 1798, *ibid.*, XXI, 450; McDonald, *The Presidency of George Washington*, 118–19; "Pacificus, No. 2," in Syrett and Cooke (eds.), *Hamilton Papers*, XV, 59.

rial support and would certainly find "the most calamitous inconveniences" to its trade if it joined France. This disproportion in itself would have rendered the treaty obligation invalid: good faith did not require that the United States hazard its very existence to secure France her American possessions (as the treaty provided for). France's intemperance had led her to her predicament and Americans were under no obligation to save France from her folly.[18]

John Quincy Adams as "Marcellus" argued in similar fashion though with different emphases. He began with an appeal to two moral authorities: Christ, who said "do unto others as you would have them do unto you," and France's Declaration of Rights, which stated "liberty consists in the power of doing whatever is not contrary to the rights of others." From these Adams concluded that morality enjoined the United States "to do nothing contrary to the rights of others." After showing that natural duty (the obligation to preserve peace), positive stipulation (treaty obligations), and economic interest (potential benefits to American commerce from war) conspired to make neutrality the proper course, Adams turned to a short discussion of the consequences of taking sides. Although he did not engage in the extensive Hamiltonian power analysis, he similarly concluded that the United States would suffer greatly if it entered the war. France's cause—"speculative freedom" become "practical tyranny"—and its conduct in the name of that cause released the United States of any moral or political obligation which the treaty with France might have enjoined: "It may be laid down as an universal principle, that no stipulation contained in a treaty, can ever oblige one nation to adopt or support the folly or injustice of another."[19]

Gratitude and the "Cause of Liberty"

Hamilton knew that France enjoyed broad popular support in the United States, most recently demonstrated by the enthusiastic reception which Genêt, the new French envoy, had received, partly out of a sense of gratitude for French aid during the Revolutionary War. The

18. "Pacificus, No. 3," in Syrett and Cooke (eds.), *Hamilton Papers*, XV, 65–69.
19. "Marcellus," in Worthington C. Ford (ed.), *The Writings of John Quincy Adams* (7 vols.; New York, 1913–17), I, 139–40.

objection that the Proclamation of Neutrality was inconsistent with gratitude sounded like an argument from morality, but Hamilton treated it as an emotional response of "all for love and world well lost." Gratitude differs from justice because gratitude is based on a benefit received or expected "which there is no right to claim," while justice is giving another his due. When benefits are bestowed for reciprocal advantages, gratitude is inoperative because payment has already been made. Thus Hamilton showed that France aided the American revolutionaries because she wanted to humble Great Britain, her great rival. Moreover, if gratitude should have any weight, Hamilton cleverly suggested, then Louis XVI, the dethroned and decapitated king of France, ought to be the beneficiary. On the whole, though, Hamilton argued that "it may be affirmed as a general principle, that the predominant motive of good offices from one nation to another is the interest or advantage of the Nation, which performs them." Following Vattel, Hamilton remarked that the rule of morality in this respect was not the same between individuals. The duty of making its own welfare the guide of its actions is much stronger on nations than on individuals. (How it defines that welfare remains an important question.) In short, a policy regulated by its own advantage, as far as justice and good faith permit, is, and ought to be, a nation's prevailing policy.[20]

Like Hamilton, Adams differentiated standards which applied to men as from those which applied to men as citizens:

> As men, we must undoubtedly lament the effusion of human blood and the mass of misery and distress which is preparing for the great part of the civilized world; but as citizens of a nation at a vast distance from the continent of Europe; of a nation whose happiness consists in a real independence, disconnected from all European politics, it is our duty to remain, all peaceable and the silent, though sorrowful spectators of the sanguinary scheme.[21]

Interestingly, Hamilton sought to salvage "the cause of liberty" as a noble goal by differentiating it from gratitude and from French monarchy. Hamilton showed that those who used gratitude as a reason to

20. "Pacificus, No. 4," in Syrett and Cooke (eds.), *Hamilton Papers*, XV, 85–86.
21. "Marcellus," in Ford (ed.), *Adams Writings*, I, 140.

act reasoned illogically; they had once praised Louis XVI for his magnanimity in supporting the Americans, but now they heaped untold abuse on his head. Those who appealed to gratitude appealed also to "the cause of liberty," yet these could work against each other. Should one be grateful to the king or should one prefer "the cause of liberty" and abandon the king to whom gratitude is owed, if it is owed at all.

Finally Hamilton addressed the timing of the proclamation. Some had argued that Washington should have held out a promise of neutrality in order to wrest concessions from the contending powers. Here too Hamilton employed a moral and political calculus in saying that to pursue such a policy would be to "display pretensions at once excessive and unprincipled." In a republic especially it was vital that citizens have a clear view of the government's position particularly in the murky waters of international affairs. To leave the position of the United States uncertain in the hope of gaining some advantages might bring on the war the public generally wished to avoid.[22]

The Argument of Americanus

As Pacificus, Hamilton was content to show what a disaster it would be for the United States to act from feelings of gratitude, but in the "Americanus" papers he returned to consider the "cause of liberty" appeal at greater length. While he believed that the proper defense of the Proclamation of Neutrality as policy rested on the executive's interpretation of the nation's positive rights and obligations based on treaties and the law of nations, in light of the nation's interests, he found that he had to address the argument from liberty, if only because of its strong popular appeal which could induce Congress to do something; the right to declare war still rested, after all, with the legislature.

There were two aspects to the question of how far regard to the cause of liberty ought to induce the United States to join the war on France's side: first, whether France's cause was truly the cause of liberty, "pursued with justice and humanity, and in a manner likely to crown it with honorable success." Second, what were the means

22. "Pacificus, No. 6," in Syrett and Cooke (eds.), *Hamilton Papers*, XV, 100–106.

available to the United States and the probable costs and benefits which would attend a policy of joining with the French? Hamilton admitted the controversial nature of the first question and disavowed the intention of entering into the discussion on this point "too complicated for the compass of these papers." Yet Hamilton, in summarizing the arguments, heavily weighted the discussion in favor of the notion that French liberty had become anarchy, and soon would become dictatorship—an astonishing prediction of Napoleon's rise. If a case could be made against the "extravagances and excesses" of the French cause which besmirched the name of liberty, then at the very least Americans ought to doubt the French claim.

On the second question, what could the United States practically contribute to the French cause and what might they expect to gain from such measures, Hamilton concluded that the United States could do very little to help: "There is no probable prospect of this country rendering material service to the cause of France, by engaging with her in the War." On the other hand, the United States would risk a great deal, perhaps its life as a nation. There were occasions, Hamilton admitted, when nations ought to hazard their existence to defend their rights and to vindicate their honor, "but let us at least have the consolation of not having rashly courted misfortune."[23]

Finally Hamilton addressed the contention that since French and American liberty were indivisible, defeat for the one would mean defeat for the other. Hamilton regarded this contention as morally and practically dubious. Morally, American liberty was founded with due respect for property, personal security, and religion. In their revolution, the Americans exercised moderation and then, "without tumult or bloodshed," adopted a form of government which established "the foundations of Liberty on the basis of Justice, Order and Law." All this stood in stark contrast with the licentiousness, anarchy, and atheism characteristic of French republicanism and Hamilton was anxious to make a clear distinction between the two. Practically, the "cause of liberty," which American Francophiles saw as indivisible, could be defeated in France but probably not in America. Should the European countries defeat France and restore the monarchy, there

23. "Americanus, No. 1" and "Americanus, No. 2," *ibid.*, XV, 678 and XVI, 14.

would be all sorts of obstacles they would have to overcome to do the same in America, not the least of which would be each other. The operation of the balance of power system in Europe and the mutual jealousy of France, Spain, and Britain would assure the Americans their independence.[24] In 1798, however, when Hamilton discussed the probability of a French invasion of America, it was because he had concluded that the French had overthrown the European system and overcome the obstacles that existed prior to the successes of the French armies in Europe. Thus Hamilton identified the balance of power system with the European system and, just as the British identified occupation of the Low Countries with a threat to British security, so Hamilton regarded French occupation of Europe as a threat to American security. The danger of identifying French and American liberty was that such an identification might create the pretext the Europeans would otherwise lack for acting against the United States. This was all the more reason to stay out of European affairs as much as possible. In short, Hamilton did not rule out the cause of liberty as a reason to fight, but he did attach a moral and prudential calculus of success as part of the decision.

Hamilton also made judgments about the probability of the success or failure of republicanism in France, which he did not include in his public discussions. In a fascinating exchange of letters with Lafayette in 1798–1799, Hamilton expressed his doubts that republicanism would succeed in France. While he did not dispute the right of the French to establish "internal liberty," he did not think that the French spirit or ethos could sustain such a government. "I shall only say that I hold with Montesquieu that a Government must be fitted to a nation as much as a Coat to the Individual, and consequently that what may be good at Philadelphia may be bad at Paris and ridiculous at Petersburgh."[25]

Hamilton demonstrated this "fitting" in the case of Santo Domingo as well. During the quasi war with France, Hamilton and

24. "Americanus, No. 2," *ibid.*, XVI, 19. Jefferson implicitly shared this view; see Samuel Flagg Bemis, *Pinckney's Treaty* (New Haven, 1960), 150–53.
25. Hamilton to Lafayette, January 6, 1799, in Syrett and Cooke (eds.), *Hamilton Papers*, XXII, 404.

Rufus King considered forming a kind of condominium with the British to remove Spain, which had made peace with France in 1795, from the Western Hemisphere. In addition to the military arrangements, some agreement would be necessary as well on the forms of government which the two countries would sponsor or guarantee in place of Spanish rule. Secretary of State Pickering raised this issue with respect to the specific case of Santo Domingo, which had just declared its independence from France under Toussaint L'Ouverture and which sought trade and recognition from the government of the United States. Pickering asked Hamilton what kind of government ought to be established there. Hamilton's reply showed that he did not think that republicanism was possible in Santo Domingo either. "No regular system of Liberty will at present suit." Instead he proposed a military government with a single executive to hold office for life, with his successor chosen by the rest of the military commanders. These recommendations reflected the feudal system which was the legacy of colonial rule in the West Indies.[26]

Both Hamilton and Adams used to advantage the double meaning of liberty as descriptive of a certain kind of regime (against tyranny) and as descriptive of desirable relations between states (against imperialism). Not all tyrannies are imperialistic, and not all empires are tyrannical, but by joining these, Hamilton and Adams put themselves on stronger ground. Parenthetically, one should note that American statesmen have galvanized public opinion most successfully when they have been able to link both descriptions of liberty— against Spain in 1898, Germany in 1917, Germany and Japan in 1941, and the Soviet Union in 1947. American attitudes toward the British Empire, on the other hand, have been more ambivalent, in part because of admiration for the British constitution, if not for its empire. By contrast, American attitudes toward the Spanish Empire were shaped by a dislike of its internal character, even though America enjoyed (and sometimes exploited) Spain's inability to project itself militarily.

---

26. Pickering to Hamilton, February 9, 1799, and Hamilton to Pickering, February 21, 1799, *ibid.*, XXII, 473–75 and 492–93.

The Jay Treaty

Having declared itself neutral in fact, if not in name, the United States still had to enforce that neutrality in the face of continued conflict in Europe. In June 1793 Britain declared France under blockade, ordered the seizure of all neutral vessels carrying contraband, including food as well as more traditional items such as arms and military supplies, and authorized the recruitment of sailors by impressment gangs. These measures bore heavily on American trade and on American seamen who were pressed into service in the British navy on the pretext that they were British deserters. Soon Jeffersonians renewed their calls for measures of commercial discrimination against Britain and in favor of France in retaliation.

When word reached the capital that the British had seized 250 American ships in one raid, the Federalists decided that more forceful measures were necessary and called for a military buildup, including the establishment of a navy, the enactment of an embargo against Britain, and the dispatch of a minister plenipotentiary to see what could be negotiated with the British. In the spring of 1794 President Washington sent John Jay to London with instructions to gain compensation for the seizures of American shipping, a commercial treaty with Great Britain, and resolution of the unexecuted points of the Anglo-American peace treaty of 1783, including the problem of British debts, the evacuation of the British posts in the Northwest Territory, and compensation for the slaves that the British army had freed or carried off during the Revolutionary War.

The treaty Jay negotiated and which Washington submitted to the Senate for ratification the following spring addressed some, but not all, of these points. In it the parties agreed to establish arbitration commissions to deal with the issues of the pre–Revolutionary War debts and compensation for illegal maritime seizures, the British agreed to give up the posts, and the British made some commercial concessions. In turn the United States gave up the right to sequester British debts, though the treaty said nothing about compensation for slaves or impressment, and the United States in effect gave up its claims to the broad definition of neutral rights. The Senate considered the treaty in secrecy and ratified it by the barest margin, but when the treaty's contents were revealed the political storm that broke was more ferocious than that over the issuance of the neutrality proclamation, because of what the treaty had given up. For Jeffersonians unfriendly to Britain, the treaty effectively created an alliance with Britain, and relinquished rights which the Americans had claimed for over fifteen years. The controversy solidified the emerging political divisions within the country and polarized the country. Once again, Hamilton took up his pen to defend the administration.[27]

The task Hamilton set for himself in defending the Jay Treaty required a much more extensive analysis, since he reviewed each article of the proposed agreement. The result was thirty-five letters entitled "The Defence" and signed "Camillus," of which ten were written by Rufus King. Like the ancient Roman hero Camillus, Hamilton was concerned about the threat of the "Gauls" to the Republic and spoke out in support of an unpopular cause. In form and in argument "The Defence" closely resembled Pacificus and Americanus. Again Hamilton defended the administration's course on legal, moral, and prudential grounds. Unlike the Pacificus essays, however, "The Defence" contained no explicit constitutional argument; that appeared late in the debate when Jeffersonians in the House, faced with the request for funds to implement the treaty, argued that separation of powers gave them the right to judge the treaty as well as the other two branches of government.[28]

Because this was a defense of a treaty, Hamilton made an even greater use of rules derived from the law of nations than he had previously. In addition to arguments that he had already made about American foreign policy, Hamilton addressed the issues of impressment, free trade, contraband, and blockades, all of which warfare in Europe had forced Americans to consider as they attempted to stay neutral. Hamilton even found himself arguing against Vattel on cer-

27. Hamilton to Washington, March 8, 1794, Hamilton to Washington, April 14, 1794, and Hamilton to Washington, April 23, 1794, *ibid.*, XVI, 130–36, 261–79, and 319–28. Hamilton to Jay, May 6, 1794, *ibid.*, XVI, 381–85, mentions neither the slave question nor impressment as objects Jay should strive for in the upcoming negotiations.
28. Douglass Adair, "A Note on Certain of Hamilton's Pseudonyms," in Colbourn (ed.), *Fame and the Founding Fathers*, 272–78.

tain points, appealing to the necessary law of nations or to modern usage which had modified European conduct since the time of Vattel. Again, Hamilton put himself on the high moral ground by advocating peace, while warning that war would surely follow if the treaty were rejected. More than that, Hamilton argued that the treaty conformed to the law of nations, served the interests of the United States, and did not violate the other treaties of the United States.

> The Treaty lately negotiated with Great Britain does nothing but confirm by a positive agreement a rule of the law of nations indicated by reason supported by the better opinion of writers ratified by modern usage— dictated by justice and good faith recognised by formal acts and declarations of different nations—witnessed by diplomatic testimony—sanctioned by our treaties with other countries and by treaties between other countries—and conformable with sound policy and the true interest of the United States.[29]

A key feature of Hamilton's approach to the Jay Treaty was his position that in the dispute with Britain over nonfulfillment of treaty obligations in the 1783 treaty there was injustice on both sides: Britain had not given up the western posts, but the United States had not secured the British debts or Loyalist property. There was no denying British infractions of the treaty or the additional problem of British depredations of American shipping in the war with France; the question at the time of sending Jay to England was how best to rectify the situation. Some had counseled measures to cut off commercial intercourse with Britain and sequester British debts, but the course taken by the administration and advocated by Hamilton was "vigorous preparation for war and one more effort to avert it by negotiation." This course was sanctioned by the law of nations, which taught that reprisals ought to be preceded with a demand for reparations and an effort to negotiate differences between countries contemplating war; the other course was fraught with danger and injustice. To threaten war through reprisals left the other party no other choice but resort to force. In addition, sending Jay gave the

29. "The Defense, No. 22," in Syrett and Cooke (ed.), *Hamilton Papers*, XIX, 394; see also Fisher Ames' speech in defense of Jay's Treaty, in Seth Ames (ed.), *The Works of Fisher Ames* (2 vols.; New York, 1971), II, 46.

United States time to fortify their ports, supply their arsenals, raise troops, and otherwise prepare for war. This course assured all that all reasonable measures had been taken to redress injuries short of war; if war came, the country would be united. Hamilton would repeat this counsel three years later during the period of quasi war with France when he supported sending an extraordinary mission to France because "as we sent an Envoy Extraordinary to Britain so ought we to send one to France." The underlying rule in both cases was that "we ought to do every thing to avoid rupture, without unworthy sacrifices, and to keep in view as a primary object union at home."[30]

One problem with the confrontational approach advanced by the Jeffersonians was its overestimate of American capabilities. To Hamilton it was a mistake to regard the United States as one of the first-rate powers of the world, and to propose action based on that assumption. The United States was in no position "to give the law to Great Britain." While the goals of the Jeffersonians on the free-ships principle, impressment, and contraband were laudable, the United States did not have the means to gain those ends. Hamilton continued to insist that peace was the real interest of the United States and ought not to be forsaken "unless the relinquishment be clearly necessary to preserve our honour on some unequivocal point, or to avoid the sacrifice of some right or interest of material and permanent importance." As a general rule derived from the law of nations, it was not until after it had become manifest that reasonable reparation of a clear, premeditated wrong could not be obtained by an amicable adjustment that honor demanded a resort to arms. This general rule anticipated the twentieth-century doctrine that efforts for pacific settlement be tried first before resorting to war.[31]

Hamilton thought the Jay Treaty had achieved real gains for the United States. First and foremost, the posts were finally going to be turned over to the United States. This would make Indian problems in the West easier to address, would prevent the British from trying

30. "The Defense, No. 2," in Syrett and Cooke (eds.), *Hamilton Papers*, XVIII, 493; Hamilton to William L. Smith, April 5, 1797, *ibid.*, XXI, 21; Alexander DeConde, *The Quasi-War: The Politics and Diplomacy of the Undeclared War with France, 1797–1801* (New York, 1966), 17–30.
31. "The Defense, No. 5," in Syrett and Cooke (eds.), *Hamilton Papers*, XIX, 90.

to create an Indian buffer state between the United States and Canada, and would attach the western lands to the United States against possible Spanish or British schemes to lure the westerners away from the United States. In addition the treaty addressed the American desire for remuneration for American shipping taken by British warships. Certainly, the United States had to make some concessions or admissions of guilt on the issue of seizure of Loyalist property, but that was the essence of the compromise which Hamilton defended. "What sensible man, what human man, will deny that a compromise which secures substantially the objects of interest is almost always preferable to war?"[32]

Hamilton refused to defend a return of Negroes carried away by the British. The established law of war gave to an enemy the use and enjoyment during war of all real property of which he obtained possession in war and the absolute ownership of all personal property which came into his hands. Personal property, as opposed to real property, could be removed as booty. The difficulty with slaves was the question of "movability," since they could be taken as booty even if they were considered real property. Vattel argued that slaves should be given back to their owners anyway and it was to him that the southerners referred on this point. Hamilton's treatment of this issue departed from this usage and his citations are derived from Vattel's discussion of prisoners of war. Whether to regard slaves first as persons or as property remained the great unresolved problem in American politics for many years to come. Hamilton also grounded his position in the law of nature, or the necessary law of nations, which held it an even greater offense to enslave men who had been promised or given their freedom than to uphold the *jus in bello* prohibition against carrying away real property. It had been wrong of the British to seduce away the slaves from their masters, but it would be even worse to return them to slavery.[33]

On the United States' side there had also been breaches of the

32. "The Defense, No. 3," *ibid.*, XVIII, 516.
33. Madison had dealt with this problem as a delegate in the Continental Congress; see his notes on debates in Boyd *et al.* (eds.), *Madison Papers*, V, 111 and 437. Hamilton's views are clear in his "Remarks on the Treaty of Amity, Commerce, and Navigation," in Syrett and Cooke (eds.), *Hamilton Papers*, XVIII, 415.

treaty and Hamilton cited a New York law which prevented Loyalist recovery of property, a South Carolina law suspending the recovery of British debts, and similar actions in Virginia. Part of this argument involved attempting to determine who had committed the first breach of the treaty. The British contended that they had retained the posts because of American breaches, whereas the Americans maintained that they had established impediments to British recovery of debts and property because of the British retention of the posts. The latter view had been brilliantly defended by Jefferson in his riposte to the British envoy, Hammond, and about the best that Hamilton could do was to establish some doubt on the point.[34]

"The Defence" is remarkable for its advocacy of the sanctity of private property, the violations of which Hamilton suggested should be avoided even during war if possible. Not only did Hamilton view hindrances to British financial activity as reprehensible, he vigorously defended the article in the treaty which stipulated compensation to British creditors for losses and damages they had suffered during and after the war, and upheld the article which prohibited the sequestration of debts as a means of reprisal. Hamilton regarded the use of sequestration as "degrading," though it, too, was sanctioned by the writers on the law of nations: "No powers of language at my command can express the abhorrence I feel at the idea of violating the property of individuals which in an authorized intercourse in time of peace has been confided to the faith of our government and laws, on account of controversies between nation and nation. In my view every moral and political sentiment unites to consign it to execration."[35]

Hamilton went on to examine in detail the right of sequestration in the opinion of jurists and in the usage of nations. What emerged from his analysis was a distinction between "rigorous" ancient practice and "lenient" modern practice, a distinction which figured prominently in many of the essays of Hume and Montesquieu. The Romans, for example, allowed this right, but since they were a warlike

34. Jefferson to Hammond, May 29, 1792, in Ford (ed.), *Jefferson Works*, VII, 9–16.
35. "The Defense, No. 18," in Syrett and Cooke (eds.), *Hamilton Papers*, XIX, 300.

115

rather than a commercial people they "carried the rights of war to an extreme not softened or humanized by the influence of commerce." The Romans even permitted the killing of foreign women and children in their midst during war: "What respect is due to maxims which have so inhuman a foundation?"

Grotius and Vattel seemed to accept the Roman precedent, though with qualifications. Their contradictory opinions reflected their ambivalence about modern principles of commerce and civil law. Hamilton based his opposition to these jurists on the grounds of the customary law and the necessary law of nations. Noting the difference between ancient and modern practice on this point, Hamilton commented: "At present in regard to the advantage and safety of commerce all the sovereigns of Europe have departed from this rigor. And as this custom has been generally received he who should act contrary to it would injure the public faith; for strangers trusted his subjects only from the firm persuasion that the general custom would be observed." Did the customary law bind the United States? Yes, through their connection with the British Empire and their acceptance of the common law. Ultimately, however, the customary law was derived from the law of nature: the obligation of nations to act with good faith to strangers who come into their midst with the understanding that they will be protected. Thus: "I derive the vindication of the article from a higher source; from the natural or necessary law of nations, from the eternal principles of morality and good faith."[36]

In addition, Hamilton argued that it was in the national interest to eschew sequestration. He assumed that commerce was advantageous to nations, but that commerce would prosper only when it was secure. A commercial country like the United States needed to retain the confidence of those it traded with by treating private property properly.[37]

---

36. "The Defense, No. 20," *ibid.*, XIX, 329–342; Patrick Henry took the opposite view, citing Vattel and Grotius, in the case of Jones v. Walker; see William Wirt (ed.), *The Speeches and Correspondence of Patrick Henry* (3 vols.; New York, 1891), II, 601–48.

37. "The Defense, No. 21," in Syrett and Cooke (eds.), *Hamilton Papers*, XIX, 372.

The distinction between ancient and modern practice extended to the definition of neutral rights as well. Vattel, in his chapter on neutrality, sanctioned the seizure of enemy property on neutral ships, provided the master of the vessel was reimbursed; he allowed the interruption of all commerce with places under siege; and he included as contraband arms, ammunition, timber for ship-building, every kind of naval stores, horses, and even provisions, in certain circumstances when famine might bring the enemy to reason. Hamilton admitted that the modern modifications of these harsh rules might be desirable but he did not believe that they were worth going to war to obtain. Even Jefferson, who supported the modern neutralist definition and argued that food should not be considered contraband, in his letter to the French government detailing American charges against Genêt, had admitted that the principle of "free ships, free goods" had not yet become a part of the established law of nations. Until Britain conceded on the point, moreover, the United States could not claim it as a right, and it would be a long time, Hamilton suspected, until the principal maritime power acceded to the new principles or until belligerent powers adhered to them in time of war.[38]

On other points, as Madison complained during the debate in the House on whether to carry out the treaty, the document relied wherever it could on Vattel's authority. The articles on contraband reproduced Vattel's list cited above and Hamilton noted that Heinecius, Bynkershoek, and Grotius could have been cited as additional authorities. Hamilton said he regretted that the rigorous law of nations had been followed rather than the modern and disputed the British construction of Vattel on the contraband list, but, he admitted, "it cannot be objected to as a departure from" the law of nations strictly defined. He took a similar view on impressment, where he disagreed with British practice, but found it difficult to conceive of a practical rule agreeable to both sides. Apparently the legal authorities

38. Vattel, Book III, Chap. 7, secs. 112–17; "The Defense, No. 31," in Syrett and Cooke (eds.), *Hamilton Papers*, XIX, 472–79; "Remarks on the Treaty of Amity," *ibid.*, XVIII, 437–40; Jefferson to Gouverneur Morris, August 16, 1793, in Andrew Lipscomb and Albert Bergh (eds.), *The Writings of Thomas Jefferson* (20 vols.; Washington, D.C., 1905), IX, 180–209.

had not dealt with this issue which concerned the unique case of two nations consisting of people who looked alike and spoke the same language.[39]

What made Hamilton's task in defending Jay's Treaty difficult was not the legal objections but rather the clear interest of the United States in obtaining broad definitions of neutral rights and the fact that the United States had asserted those definitions in the treaties it had written following independence. Hamilton's views, then, represented an important retrenchment of United States policy and his use of the law of nations could not disguise this. As a result several American treaties with other countries would have to be renegotiated to reflect this narrower interpretation of American rights.[40]

The political storm over the Jay Treaty was very much in President Washington's mind as he delivered his Farewell Address. As the fullest and official expression of the Federalist interpretation of the American consensus, the Farewell Address contained most of the themes articulated by Hamilton and Adams. There was an appeal to allow reason rather than sentiment—"inveterate antipathies against particular nations and passionate attachment for others"—to govern the nation's foreign policy. It asserted the great rule of conduct in foreign policy as having as little political connection as possible with European nations, out of duty and out of interest. It suggested that American politics was superior to that of Europe by virtue of its moderation, and Washington held up the example of American prudence and sober republicanism at odds with European "ambition, rivalship, interest, humor, and caprice," a division of political spheres also found later in the Monroe Doctrine. Finally it noted the need for a respectable defensive posture and held out the prospect that in the future the United States would have the power to defend its neutral rights. Some day the United States might gain a safe preponderance of power in a global balance of power system able, in the words of

39. "Speech on Jay's Treaty," Gaillard Hunt (ed.), *The Writings of James Madison* (9 vols.; New York, 1900–10), VI, 286; "The Defense, No. 33," in Syrett and Cooke (eds.), *Hamilton Papers*, XIX, 508.
40. Gregg L. Lint, "The American Revolution and the Law of Nations, 1776–1789," *Diplomatic History*, I (Winter, 1977), 20–34; Samuel F. Bemis, *John Quincy Adams and the Foundations of American Foreign Policy* (New York, 1949), 87–106.

118

Federalist Number 11, "to dictate the terms of the connection between the old and the new world!" Until then, the United States might have to form temporary alliances out of necessity, and Hamilton undoubtedly saw his accommodations to British power in that light.[41]

The Quasi War with France

Hamilton saw his country as unable, out of insufficient cause or weakness, to become involved in war in 1790, 1793, or 1795, but by 1798 he had changed his mind. This change was prompted by a) French attacks on American shipping, b) continued French pretensions to universal empire, and c) the threat of French occupation of Louisiana and invasion of the southern United States. Hamilton made these points in a series of articles written in March and April of 1798 and entitled "The Stand." Having warned his countrymen of the danger, Hamilton characteristically called for a state of "mitigated hostility" in which the United States took measures to arm itself while at the same time pursuing one last effort to negotiate with the French. "My plan ever is to combine energy with moderation," he wrote a friend.[42]

In the naval contest with Britain, France found herself unable to act without violating neutral shipping. Indeed, the principle of "free ships make free goods," which had been part of the 1778 treaty with the United States, had been laid aside as early as May 9, 1793. By 1798 the French considered every neutral ship engaged in the British carrying trade a help to England and therefore an enemy to France and liable to capture. France's American supporters had been embarrassed by this abandonment, though they blamed the Jay Treaty for making it necessary for the French to resort to such measures. Hamilton doubted that this principle could become part of the customary law of nations, so he did not dwell on these violations, except as an infringement of American rights generally.

41. Washington's Farewell Address may be found in Richardson (ed.), *Compilation*, I, 213–24; Hamilton, Jay, and Madison, *The Federalist Papers*, 91; Stourzh, *Alexander Hamilton and the Idea of Republican Government*, 194–200.
42. Hamilton to William L. Smith, April 5, 1798, in Syrett and Cooke (eds.), *Hamilton Papers*, XXI, 21.

Hamilton concentrated instead on the danger of France's "pretensions to universal empire," about which he had warned earlier. He repeated many of the points made in the Pacificus and Americanus essays. France had prostrated surrounding nations, sought universal empire, decreed war against all monarchies, and invited sedition in every country, all of which were violations of the law of nations and a threat to the balance of power system. Hamilton clearly believed that the coalitions against France fought in a just cause:

> The moment the convention vomited forth those venomous decrees, all the governments were justifiable in making war. There is no rule of public law better established or on better grounds, than that whenever one nation unequivocally avows maxims of conduct dangerous to the security and tranquility of others, they have a right to attack her, and to endeavor to disable her from carrying her schemes into effect.[43]

Hamilton clearly sided with Britain and her claims that she acted not only in self-defense but in defense of the European balance as a whole. Britain, to be sure, had used this claim to advance her own position in international politics, but it was no less true that she had also been "an essential and an effectual shield against real danger." This was a theme which Federalists like Fisher Ames would stress even more strongly than Hamilton had. In an essay entitled "The Balance of Europe," Ames maintained,

> The British navy, considered in an abstract point, is too large and too superior to that of all other nations, especially our own. But naval power, it may be said, is rather less fitted for the purposes of national aggrandizement than any other. It is very likely to provoke enemies and not well adapted to subdue them. . . . If it be an evil for that navy to be so great, it is clearly a less evil than for the French power to be freed from its resistance. Remove that resistance, and France would rule the civilized world.[44]

Hamilton did more than describe French violations of the public law of Europe; he had come to the conclusion that French principles themselves must be attacked. Where Vattel had written that religion

---

43. "The Stand," No. 2, *ibid.*, XXI, 395.
44. "The Stand," No. 4, *ibid.*, 413; "Balance of Europe," in Ames (ed.), *Works of Fisher Ames*, II, 234.

120

ought not to enter into discussions of international politics, Hamilton introduced it. He had started to move in this direction in his earlier writings, but in "The Stand" he went much further than he had before. To Theodore Sedgwick he wrote privately, "We must oppose to political fanaticism religious zeal." He did this in two ways. First he discussed the effort among the French to destroy all religious opinion "and to pervert a whole people to atheism." For Hamilton religion and morality were closely linked, and he saw in the loss of religion in France the loss of morality as well; only the terrors of despotism would be able to curb the impetuous passions of man, and to confine him within the bounds of social duty. Secondly Hamilton called for a day of national fasting and prayer, which would presumably call attention to the differences between French and American liberty on the subject of religion. This new sensitivity to the political uses of religion found its ultimate conclusion in Hamilton's proposals for a "Christian Constitutional Society" which would compete with the Jeffersonian party and its "Jacobin" principles.[45]

It was only after this discussion of the French threat to the European system and to the religious dimension of civilized life that Hamilton treated French relations with the United States. Simply that France was conducting an unjust war did not mean that the United States had to enter into a coalition against her; that was clear from the distinction between the necessary and the voluntary laws of nature. However, French actions did have a direct effect on the United States about which the United States was obligated to take steps. Hamilton mentioned several concerns: French violations of American shipping, its high-handed treatment of American envoys, and its continuing aspirations in North America. The latter seemed to worry him the most. The French, by virtue of their dominance over Spain, might easily force the Spanish to cede Louisiana back to them; this effort had been widely rumored and subsequent historical research

45. Hamilton to Sedgwick, March 15, 1798, and "The Stand, No. 3," in Syrett and Cooke (eds.), *Hamilton Papers*, XXI, 363 and 402–405; Hamilton to James Bayard, April 16–21, *ibid.*, XXV, 605–10; Douglass Adair and Marvin Harvey, "Was Alexander Hamilton a Christian Statesman?" in Colbourn (ed.), *Fame and the Founding Fathers*, 141–59. For an earlier reference linking morality and religion see Washington's Farewell Address, in Richardson (ed.), *Compilation*, I, 219.

has established the French desire to regain Louisiana. Conceivably, even if the Spanish refused to forfeit the lands, the French might be in a position to take the territories by force, since the Spanish garrisons were known to be weak.[46]

Hamilton seems to have considered the possibility of invasion by France to be very real. This was something that not even all the Federalists believed, and that the Jeffersonians ridiculed. Hamilton's case went as follows: France had real claims in North America, indigenous support in Louisiana, Canada, and the United States, and bases in the Caribbean from which a military expedition could be launched. The most substantial obstacle to such a plan would, of course, be the British navy, but France under Napoleon could overcome it either by forcing Britain to negotiate a peace treaty with France, leaving France free to conduct a campaign in North America, or by successfully invading Britain and neutralizing the British navy that way. For Hamilton, then, it was possible that the United States could be left to contend alone with the conqueror of Europe. Hamilton tried to use to advantage all of the wrong predictions made about the probable course of the war: the French triumphs in Europe had confounded and astonished the world and suggested that anything was possible.

While many Federalists conceded the possibility of a French invasion, they regarded it as rather remote. Washington, for example, wrote Hamilton that he was undecided about the prospects of an invasion, but he thought that Hamilton underestimated the strength of the United States. However, the publication of the infamous "X, Y, Z" papers which revealed French efforts to bribe the special American negotiators united the country in a wave of indignation. Congress responded by creating a new navy and raising a new army with Washington and Hamilton at the head, abrogating the Franco-American treaties of 1778, suspending commerce with France, and

46. Frederick Jackson Turner, "The Policy of France Toward the Mississippi Valley in the Period of Washington and Adams," 249–79, and "The Origin of Genêt's Projected Attack on Louisiana and the Floridas," *American Historical Review*, III (July, 1897), 650–71; James A. James, "French Opinion as a Factor in Preventing War Between France and the United States," *American Historical Review*, XXX (October, 1924), 44–55.

authorizing American armed ships to protect American commerce and to capture armed French vessels. Fearful of an Anglo-American alliance and hopeful of retaining its colonial empire in the Western Hemisphere, the French sought to renew negotiations.

Without consulting other Federalist leaders still eager for war, President Adams decided that yet another effort at negotiations should be made. This move helped to split the Federalists and prepared the way for Jefferson's election in 1800. The treaty which resulted from the renewed negotiations, the Convention of Mortefontaine, signed in September 1800, canceled the 1778 treaty but retained the principle of broad neutral rights. Hamilton interpreted this as a continuation of the French strategy to create friction between the United States and Great Britain, but urged acceptance of the convention for fear of what a Jefferson administration might try to negotiate with the French instead.[47]

Hamilton saw in the possibility of war with France an opportunity as well as a danger. In a letter to Harrison Gray Otis in early 1799, Hamilton revealed, "I have been long in the habit of considering the acquisition of those countries [Louisiana and the Floridas] as essential to the permanency of the Union, which I consider as very important to the welfare of the whole."[48] Gilbert Lycan has detailed how Hamilton attempted to prepare for the acquisition of those territories by building up military forces in the West. In the event of a war with France, which plausibly might include Spain, a military expedition under the command of General Wilkinson, in consultation with Hamilton and other government leaders, would be ready to descend the Mississippi and occupy New Orleans. Little came of these plans, however. Secretary of the Treasury Wolcott doubted that the United

---

47. Washington to Hamilton, May 27, 1798, in Syrett and Cooke (eds.), *Hamilton Papers*, XXI, 470–74; "France and America," Hamilton to Sedgwick, December 12, 1800, and Hamilton to Morris, December 24, 1800, *ibid.*, XXV, 131–39, 269–70, and 271–73. On the breach in Federalist ranks see "Letter Concerning the Public Conduct and Character of John Adams," *ibid.*, XXV, 169–234; for a detailed account of the quasi war see DeConde, *The Quasi-War*.
48. Hamilton to Otis, January 26, 1799, in Syrett and Cooke (eds.), *Hamilton Papers*, XXI, 440–42.

States had the means to support a venture whose costs were unpredictable, and President Adams was more desirous of reducing tensions with France than of possibly gaining Louisiana.[49]

Would a military expedition to take New Orleans have conformed to Vattel's just-war criteria? So long as Louisiana remained in the hands of the Spanish there would have been no just cause to initiate such a venture without a formal declaration by Spain. Once the French gained possession of it, however, circumstances would have changed. It was on hearing that such a transaction had taken place in 1802 that President Jefferson threatened to make an alliance with Britain. That was the course which Vattel had honored most in his discussion on the question of resorting to war for "mere increase of power," but because of Hamilton's conviction that France had engaged on a course of universal empire, Hamilton would have advocated military preparation in addition to the shift suggested by Jefferson. In fact, Hamilton's response to the news that Spain had ceded Louisiana back to France was that the United States should at once seize the Floridas and New Orleans and then negotiate.

Summary

From the foregoing discussion several conclusions may now be drawn about the Hamiltonian approach and legacy.

1. Hamilton is rightly interpreted as a defender of the national interest, but it is worth recalling how he defined it. Perhaps befitting a military man, Hamilton put a high value on the possession of strategic assets. He proved willing to sacrifice broad neutral rights to gain the posts along the Canadian border; he advocated war with France partly with a view to military occupation of New Orleans; and he recommended the protection of infant industries to make the United States more self-sufficient in manufactured goods. Each of these meant the sacrifice or nonassertion of other interests: broad neutral rights, commercial privileges, impressment, and commercial independence of Britain.

49. Lycan, *Alexander Hamilton and American Foreign Policy*, 373–94; "For the *Evening Post*," in Syrett and Cooke (eds.), *Hamilton Papers*, XXVI, 82–85.

2. The trade-off of forts for broad neutral rights also reflected Hamilton's assessment of the United States as a relatively weak state which did not have the means to achieve a broader interpretation of the national interest. At times, this assessment worked against Hamilton, as in 1799 when Treasury Secretary Wolcott argued that the nation did not have the means to undertake a conflict with the French, or when he greeted the huge Louisiana Purchase with concern because he did not think it could be adequately defended.

3. Hamilton miscalculated the extent to which the measures he proposed would divide the country. His constitutional views, financial measures, and political doctrines generated great opposition and contributed to the view that he wanted to transform the government into a monarchy on the British model. As a result Hamilton came to be seen as a party leader; this made it difficult for him to defend or reject policy without such action being interpreted in partisan ways.

4. Hamilton's military orientation seems already to have been out of step with the American national character. Commentators have often noted in the American character a generic pacifism, which turns into crusaderism when war does come. As long as Hamilton identified peace as the best course for the United States he exploited and perhaps contributed to the pacifist strain. The greatest opposition to Hamilton occurred when he advocated "mitigated hostilities" with France and the application of force in Louisiana. His advocacy of an expanded and regular army which could put down domestic "Whiskey Rebellions" as well as meet foreign threats could only be met with suspicion by Americans still familiar with Britain's standing armies.

5. Hamilton relied greatly on Vattel and the other authorities of the law of nations as he endeavored to lead the country in its foreign policy and to persuade his fellow citizens of the correctness of his course. Stephen Rosen has pointed out that Hamilton could do this because the law of nations reflected international reality: "By demanding that American citizens obey international law, Hamilton was demanding that they obey the reality of external powers."[50] Ac-

50. Stephen Rosen, "Alexander Hamilton and the Domestic Uses of International Law," *Diplomatic History*, V (Summer, 1981), 195–96.

quiescence in the British interpretation of belligerent rights rather than the broad neutralist definition was one consequence of this view. On the other hand, without the maintenance of a balance of power system in Europe even the limited rights and choices of the weaker powers would disappear.

CHAPTER V

The Jeffersonian
Approach

Opponents of the Federalist world view offered a quite different interpretation of republican government and of American foreign policy. Under the leadership of Thomas Jefferson and James Madison this interpretation came to supplant Federalism with the election of 1800. The republicanism these men espoused included themes quite different from those of the Federalists and incorporated many of the concerns of the Anti-Federalists. Jeffersonianism included fear of executive aggrandizement, distrust of standing armies (which for some extended to a distrust of the navy), confidence in the yeoman farmer as the bulwark of American liberty, an emphasis on economy in government, reliance on local administration, advocacy of economic sanctions and commercial policy as a tool of foreign policy, and a warm feeling for the French.[1] For the Jeffersonians, the greatest threat to American interests and security came from the British; they rejected, however, the Hamiltonian approach as appeasement and counseled instead continued use of the French alliance as a counterweight to British power. This approach had worked in the American Revolutionary War and they saw no reason why it would not continue to work to check British power and moderate British practice in trade, navigation, and neutral rights.

In taking this view the Jeffersonians also accepted the arguments of

1. All of these themes save the last may be found in Jefferson's First Inaugural Address, in Richardson (ed.), *Compilation*, I, 309–12.

eighteenth-century French publicists who insisted, especially after the French defeat in the Seven Years' War, that it was the British Empire which represented the gravest threat to the balance of power system. Mirabeau, Moreau, Donois, and Vauban all argued that Britain's mastery of the seas, its vast colonial holdings, and its monopoly of trade ought to be brought into the scales of the European balance, which would then reveal Britain's preponderance. The idea of a balance ought to be extended to colonies, trade, and sea power, they contended; otherwise Britain's uncontested mastery of the seas would become mastery of the coasts and finally mastery of the European continent. Where the English had once championed the freedom of the seas to undermine Spanish dominance, the French took up the cause in the mid–eighteenth century; where the British had claimed the mantle of the "holder of the balance," the French laid claim to the guardianship of Europe. Adolph Rein has perceptively suggested that the three great ideas of freedom, equality, and fraternity advanced by the French revolutionaries appeared first in connection with the great foreign policy confrontation with England as *freedom* of the seas and of trade, *equality* of trade, power, shipping, and colonial wealth, and *fraternity* of states in Europe and America against the British colossus.[2]

These views attracted the Americans, who understood that they could gain much if these principles prevailed. Their contribution would be to detach themselves from Britain and direct more of their trade to the other European states; this would reduce British power and distribute trade more equitably. Jefferson had played a crucial role in both efforts, though his efforts to build a Franco-American commercial system were out of proportion to the results obtained.[3]

Since the law of nations pertaining to trade and neutral rights largely reflected British dominance of the seas, the French and the Americans contended for changes in the law of nations as well as for redistribution of power and trade. While Hamilton generally stopped with Vattel in his interpretation of the law of nations, the Jefferson-

2. Adolph Rein, "Über die Bedeutung der Überseeischen Ausdehnung für das europaische Staatensystem," *Historische Zeitschrift*, CXXXVII (1927), 62–68.
3. Merrill Peterson, "Thomas Jefferson and Commercial Policy, 1783–1793," *William and Mary Quarterly*, 3rd ser., XXII (October, 1965), 584–610.

ians strove to go beyond him. Jefferson and Madison understood the link between the law of nations and the distribution of power, but for the most part they were frustrated in their attempts to manipulate the European balance to effect changes in the law of nations. One reason why they objected so vociferously to Hamilton's policy was that it drew back from the attempt to challenge British power and the effort to sustain the broad neutralist interpretation of their rights. The Jeffersonians, however, persisted in this effort and seemed to believe even Napoleon's protestations that he was fighting for the freedom of the seas and broad neutral rights, just as many of the European neutrals seemed to accept the Napoleonic argument that the Continental System was necessary to break the British monopoly of trade. Jefferson never seriously accepted the notion that no matter how offensive Britain's actions toward the United States, Britain was fighting a war against an aggressor bent on world conquest. Indeed, several of the measures which Jefferson took as president, designedly or not, clearly favored France.[4]

Jefferson's approach has been variously described as ideological blindness or as a realistic assertion of the national interest; it also implies a certain view of the European balance. Like Hamilton, Jefferson understood the importance to American security of an equilibrium in Europe, yet, unlike Hamilton, he seemed very optimistic about the resiliency of the European system. To put it another way, Jefferson pressed the assertion of broad neutral rights as vital national interests against the British even to the point of risking final French victory. As Vattel's discussion of the balance of power system suggests, sometimes there may occur tensions between the assertion of national interests and the maintenance of the balance of power system, where some sacrifice of short-term interest for a longer-term interest in general stability ought to occur. Hamilton's acquiescence to the British view on neutral rights reflected his doubt that the broad definition could ever be sustained in war and his conviction that the

4. Lawrence J. Kaplan, "Jefferson, the Napoleonic Wars, and the Balance of Power," *William and Mary Quarterly*, 3d ser., XIV (April, 1957), 197; Henry Adams, *History of the United States Under the Administrations of Jefferson and Madison* (9 vols.; New York, 1962), IV, 396; Timothy Pickering, *Letters Addressed to People of the United States* (London, 1811).

British were maintaining the European balance on which American security depended; Jefferson expressed concern about the French threat to the European system only very late in Napoleon's career.[5]

Jeffersonians, then, saw two threats to the American republic in the Hamiltonian system: first, the subversion of republican government properly understood, and second, the appeasement of Britain which required the sacrifice of some American rights and interests. These concerns came together in the willingness of Jeffersonians, at the rhetorical level at least, to make the internal regimes of other states a consideration in the making of American foreign policy.

Jefferson and the Nootka Sound Crisis

Jefferson's cabinet opinion on the Nootka Sound crisis and his subsequent instructions to William Carmichael, the American envoy in Spain, provide the best example of the Jeffersonian strategic outlook. With the threat of war between Spain and Britain, Jefferson was deeply impressed with the magnitude of the threat to the United States if Britain should take Louisiana and the Floridas from Spain. British possession of these lands would complete British encirclement of the United States and allow the British even greater control of American markets. The United States had benefited from the check on British power provided by the Spanish, and "should view with extreme uneasiness any attempts of either power to seize the possessions of the other on our frontier, as we consider our own safety interested in a due balance between our neighbors." If war against Britain was the only means to prevent this, then he would advise war. Nevertheless, that step could be deferred until the threat was more immediate: "I am for preserving neutrality as long, and entering into the war as late, as possible." With France and Spain allies, the United States could join them, if necessary, to defeat the British. The present course for the United States, however, was to avoid offending either party; the Americans were within their rights to refuse passage, though if they chose to grant it, they would have to

5. Kaplan, "Jefferson, the Napoleonic Wars, and the Balance of Power," 204; Jefferson to Thomas Lieper, August 21, 1807, in Ford (ed.), *Jefferson Works*, IX, 129–30.

extend that right to both parties. Jefferson agreed with Hamilton that if the United States refused Britain and yet the British marched through American territory, the United States must either enter into war immediately or "pocket an acknowledged insult." Jefferson preferred no answer at all. In that case, if the British marched, there was no dishonor and the British would plead military necessity, so the Spanish would have no grounds for complaint.[6]

Jefferson saw in the crisis a chance to allow Spain to pay for American neutrality. Like Hamilton, he had his eyes on the Mississippi and on a port for western American farmers. While Hamilton thought that these would be gained only by confronting Spain, probably in some sort of cooperation with England, Jefferson hoped to use the crisis to persuade Spain to give up part of her American holdings in return for an American guaranty of the rest. In his instructions to Carmichael, Jefferson asserted American rights to the use of the Mississippi and laid out the options available to the Americans to get it: force or negotiation. If the Americans chose force, Jefferson asserted that New Orleans could easily be taken; they could also act in concert with Britain and divide the spoils. Jefferson rejected such an entente, however, because "it may eventually lead us into embarrassing situations with our best friend—France." Jefferson preferred a negotiated solution and offered the Spanish arguments to show them why they ought to prefer a settlement with the Americans. Jefferson characteristically resorted to internal regime criteria to argue that the Spanish Empire would be safer with American than with British neighbors. Britain's governing principles were "Conquest, Colonization, Commerce, and Monopoly," and no part of Spain's American empire would be safe if the British were allowed in. On the other hand, the Americans held to principles of government which were hostile to conquest and it would not be in the interest of the Americans to cross the Mississippi for some time to come.

Jefferson played out the consequences of this arrangement for Spain; Spain would obtain American support and secure its posses-

6. Jefferson to Madison, July 12, 1790, and "First Opinion of the Secretary of State," August 28, 1790, in Boyd (ed.), *Jefferson Papers*, XVII, 110 and 129–30. For similar sentiments on the importance of having balanced powers on America's borders see "Opinion of the Chief Justice," *ibid.*, 134–37.

sions; an agreement would bring the Americans in on the French and Spanish side in case of war with Britain; and American privateers could do extensive damage to British shipping. "By withholding supplies of provisions, as well as by concurring in expeditions, the British islands will be in imminent danger." Jefferson had seen the French naval buildup in the mid-1780s and he evidently believed that the United States could tip the balance against Britain; at least this is the proposition that he held out to the Spanish.[7]

Unfortunately by the time these instructions arrived in Spain, the Spanish were moving toward war with France and alliance with Britain. This was a turn of events which Jefferson had not anticipated and which made his strategy inapplicable. By 1795, however, the Spanish and the French were negotiating peace terms and the Spanish were again concerned with British aspirations in the Western Hemisphere. The Jay mission to Britain provoked the fear in the Spanish that Jay was making an alliance with the British to attack Spanish territories; this fear resulted in the Treaty of San Lorenzo or Pinckney's Treaty in which the Spanish acceded to the navigation and boundary claims of the United States in order to keep the United States neutral. This treaty substantially vindicated Jefferson's strategy on the Mississippi valley questions, although ironically, Jeffersonians were the ones who resisted the Jay mission and the subsequent Jay Treaty. They did not think it necessary to enter into what they regarded as a de facto alliance with Britain to provide the necessary incentives to induce the Spanish to yield. When, as president, Jefferson endeavored to gain the Floridas from Spain, he did make vague threats of cooperation with Britain; but his main strategy focused on persuading the French to encourage their Spanish allies to turn the land over to the Americans.[8]

The Argument of Helvidius

Jefferson opposed the broad construction of the neutrality proclamation on the grounds on which Hamilton chose to defend it: its con-

7. "Outline of Policy on the Mississippi Question," in Boyd *et al.* (eds.), *Jefferson Papers*, XVII, 114–16; Bowman, "Jefferson, Hamilton, and American Foreign Policy," 18–30.
8. Adams, *History*, III, 61–161 *passim*.

stitutionality, legality, morality, and prudence. He wrote Madison several times in mid-1793 about the proclamation, indicating that he thought that the executive had insufficient authority to declare treaties suspended or guaranties inoperative. Madison took up this theme at great length in his response to Pacificus as "Helvidius," prepared at Jefferson's insistence.

The strength of Madison's discussion of the constitutional issue raised by the proclamation lay in his definitions of executive and legislative power and in his understanding of human nature, which made broad grants of authority undesirable. The legislative power, "an integral and pre-eminent" part of sovereignty, makes the laws, and the executive executes or carries them into effect. Since treaties and declarations of war have the character of law, they are the natural province of the legislative power. These powers are not exceptional grants of power, executive in nature, especially placed in the legislature by the Constitution, as Pacificus had suggested. With the right to take these actions goes the right to judge whether these actions ought to be made. These rights, by definition, and by the Constitution, lie with the legislature. "Can the inference be avoided, that the executive, instead of a similar right to judge is as much excluded from the right to judge as from the right to declare?" Having found no basis in the Constitution for the kind of claims made by Pacificus in either the separation of powers, the commander-in-chief clause, the take-care clause, the removal power, or the right to receive ambassadors, Madison proceeded to a discussion of the danger which Pacificus' teaching posed for republican liberty.[9]

Repeating in more picturesque terms what he had said in the constitutional debates, Madison declared that "war is the nurse of executive aggrandizement." If the expansive doctrine defended by Pacificus took root in the public mind, other broad claims by the executive would follow and the likelihood of war increase. The eventual outcome would be to transform the American republic into a monarchy.[10] Madison here made the domestic consequences of war an im-

9. "Helvidius, No. 2," in Hunt (ed.), *Madison Writings*, VI, 153; Henkin, *Foreign Affairs and the Constitution*, 82–85.

10 "Helvidius, No. 4," in Hunt (ed.), *Madison Writings*, VI, 174–75; Farrand (ed.) *The Records of the Federal Convention*, II, 318 and 540.

portant criterion in considering whether to resort to force. In the words of Henry Adams, "The dread of war, radical in Republican theory, sprang not so much from the supposed waste of life or resources as from the retroactive effects which war must exert on the form of government."[11]

Underlying Madison's concern was an appeal to the generally accepted assumption of a universal law of human corruption through power characteristic of radical Whig thought and later summarized so memorably by Lord Acton. Madison did not trust human nature when put in positions of authority, particularly without built-in restraints. Too much power in the hands of a single man was dangerous: that was the defect of monarchy. The expansive doctrine of presidential power relied too heavily on the assumption that a single individual with unchecked power would work to promote the common good. Here Madison cleverly cited a passage from *Federalist* Number 75, written by Hamilton, which defended the sharing of the treaty-making power between the president and the Senate on similar grounds: "The history of human conduct does not warrant that exalted opinion of human virtue, which would make it wise in a nation to commit interests of so delicate and momentous a kind, as those which concern its intercourse with the rest of the world, to the sole disposal of a magistrate created and circumstanced as would be a president of the United States."[12]

If Pacificus' doctrine took hold, Madison predicted, the current bias toward peace by the executive would become bias toward war, as ambitious presidents learned how much war works in their favor. In an article on Rousseau's proposals for perpetual peace, written for the *National Gazette* a year and a half earlier, Madison had already addressed himself to this problem at some length. There he divided war into two classes: diplomatic wars—those that flow from the "mere will of the government"—and popular wars—those that accord with the will of society itself. He attributed the past frequency of wars to a "will in the government independent of the will of the people," implying that wars would be much less frequent if every

11. Adams, *History*, IV, 273.
12. Hamilton, Jay, and Madison, *The Federalist Papers*, 451.

government subjected its will to that of society. So long as the decision for war depended on those whose ambition, greed, or caprice could be set against and dominate the community; so long as war was declared by those who spend the public money and not by those whose taxes filled the treasury; so long as it was decided by those who directed the military rather than by those who had to fight; and so long as it was decided by those whose power would be enhanced by war, "the disease [of war] must continue to be *hereditary* like the government of which it is the offspring."[13]

The starting point, then, of any program to promote perpetual peace would be to replace monarchical governments with popular governments. This at least would reduce the occasions of diplomatic war. How probable was it that popular governments would replace monarchies? Madison did not say, nor did he say that the United States ought to make it a goal or policy to spread popular governments. He did say that perpetual peace would probably never be more than a vision, but he did hold out some hope based on the examples of the American and French constitutions. By those constitutions the executive was made subordinate to or the same with the will of the people through their elected representatives; an executive who felt free to go beyond the bounds of the law would be separating the government from the will of the people. Such an executive would feel free to engage in those diplomatic wars so characteristic of European balance of power politics and in this come to resemble those European monarchs. As put by Helvidius:

> In war, a physical force is to be created; and it is the executive will, which is to direct it. In war, the public treasuries are to be unlocked; and it is to be the executive hand which is to dispense them. In war, honors, and emoluments of office are to be multiplied; and it is the executive patronage under which they are to be enjoyed. It is in war, finally, that laurels are to be gathered; and it is the executive brow which they are to encircle.[14]

---

13. "Universal Peace," in Hunt (ed.), *Madison Writings*, VI, 89. Jefferson was even more outspoken about the tendency of monarchs to resort to war; see Jefferson to John Rutledge, August 6, 1787, in Boyd *et al.* (eds.), *Jefferson Papers*, XI, 700–701, and Jefferson to William Duane, August 4, 1812, in Ford (ed.), *Jefferson Works*, XI, 365–67.
14. "Helvidius, No. 4," in Hunt (ed.), *Madison Writings*, VI, 174.

Rather than rely on the judgment of monarchs to act in their interests and therefore seek limited aims, Madison sought to restrict the resort to force even more than had Vattel. Significantly, Madison concerned himself throughout this discussion with the *frequency* of war rather than the *moderation* of war.

Where did this doctrine of executive power come from? asked Madison. He found the answer in the theory and practice of the British government, against which a war had just been fought. "The power of making treaties and the power of declaring war are *royal* prerogatives in the *British* government, and accordingly treated as executive prerogatives by *British* commentators." Madison no doubt expected to score with this accusation, given broad suspicions of and even hatred of British power. Nevertheless, there was more to Madison's argument than anti-British invective; he was endeavoring to establish a specifically republican executive quite distinct from a monarchy. Accordingly Madison dismissed Vattel's, Locke's, and Montesquieu's expositions of executive power because they all wrote "with their eyes too much on monarchical governments, where all powers are confounded in the sovereignty of the prince." [15]

Madison reinforced this distinction between American and European politics and executives in another article for the *National Gazette* entitled "Spirit of Governments." Montesquieu in discussing this topic had reduced the operative principles of various forms of government to fear in despotisms, honor in monarchies, and virtue in republics. Madison offered his own, different, typology as follows: first, governments that operate by permanent military force which at once maintains the government and is maintained by it; second, governments that operate by corrupt influence; and third, governments that derive their energy from the will of the society and act in the interests of that society. Almost every country of Europe, "the quarter of the globe which calls itself the pattern of civilization and the pride of humanity," subjected its people to the burdens of military rule. Madison's typology took advantage of the widespread distrust

15. "Helvidius, No. 1," *ibid.*, 144 and 150; Ruth Weissbourd Grant and Stephen Grant, "The Madisonian Presidency," in Joseph Bessette and Jeffrey Tulis (eds.), *The Presidency in the Constitutional Order* (Baton Rouge, 1980), 31–64.

of standing armies which was part of radical Whig thought and which had been one reason for the American Revolution. On the other hand, "it is the glory of America to have invented, and her unrivalled happiness to possess" a republican government which operated by virtue of the will of society. That achievement must be preserved and the nation's institutions must permit its preservation.[16]

Madison was less sanguine about the possibilities of preventing popular wars; indeed it seems clear that if there was to be war Madison wanted it to be a popular war. Nevertheless he did suggest that to curb the popular appetite for war, legislators ought to enact laws which would subject the will of society to the reason of society.[17] This would be done by requiring that war be declared by the people's representatives in the legislature and ensuring that the generation which wanted war be required to bear the burdens of that war as fully as possible. Madison meant here the financial burden, which governments were prone to pass along to succeeding generations in the form of perpetual debts. This was not a new argument and Madison drew on some of the points that Hume had made about the perils of borrowing to fund wars. Jeffersonian adherence to militias as against standing or professional armies and to economic sanctions as an instrument of policy reinforces the conclusion that Madison wanted a war, if there was to be one, to bear on the whole nation. This is the logic of the reliance on citizen-soldiers, economic sanctions, and legislative declarations of war; it tends to lead of course to total war, quite at variance with the just-war/limited-war tradition in which Vattel and Hamilton placed themselves.

This is clear as well in Jefferson's democratic interpretation of Vattel on the nature of treaties, which Madison reviewed in Helvidius. Here the two men contested the legality of the proclamation in the law of nations. Hamilton had contended that the treaty was personal in nature and therefore nonbinding, but Jefferson argued that it had been made in the name of the French people whose agent at the time

16. "Spirit of Governments," in Hunt (ed.), *Madison Writings*, VI, 94; Jefferson offered a somewhat similar typology in Jefferson to Madison, January 30, 1787, in Boyd *et al.* (eds.), *Jefferson Papers*, XI, 92–93.
17. "Universal Peace," in Hunt (ed.), *Madison Writings*, VI, 89.

the king happened to be. Since the people are the source of authority in the nation they have the right to change their form of government and, as Hamilton himself conceded, real treaties remained binding despite changes in government.

Madison likewise insisted that all treaties are real unless the treaty expressly states otherwise. With a citation to Vattel and to Burlamaqui, Madison maintained that though a nation may change its organs of government, it could not disengage itself from treaties that had been made. (This point worked against the French as much as against Hamilton because the French revolutionaries had renounced the treaties which the monarchy had made.) On another point of the law of nations, again with a citation to Vattel, Madison complained that the administration had not given France a fair hearing on the meaning of the guaranty. According to Vattel, neither side had the right to interpret a treaty at its own pleasure: "To decide a question of fact, as well as of principle, without waiting for such representations and proofs as the absent and interested party might have to produce, would have been a proceeding contrary to the ordinary maxims of justice." [18]

Hamilton had argued in the cabinet that according to Vattel a treaty could be broken if it proved self-destructive, dangerous, or useless. Jefferson disputed the suggestion that the French treaty was dangerous and rejected the reading of Vattel which permitted the nonperformance of treaty obligations on the grounds of mere uselessness or disagreeability. The danger from France was remote and too uncertain to nullify the treaties. In his brief to Washington, Jefferson cited the opinions of Grotius, Pufendorf, and Wolff to show that the authorities on the law of nations insisted that "treaties remain obligatory notwithstanding any change in the form of government, except in the single case where the preservation of that form was the object of the treaty." Only Vattel went on to admit that a treaty's uselessness or annoyance would permit a state to renounce it, and this put him against the other writers and "the morality of every honest man." Besides, Jefferson contended that Vattel had been mis-

18. "Helvidius, No. 3 and Helvidius, No. 5," *ibid.*, 164 and 185.

interpreted and he produced a long citation in which Vattel underscored the obligation to keep one's commitments. From this "who will doubt that treaties are of the things sacred among nations?"[19]

Vattel taught that the law of nature applied differently to individuals and to states because of their different natures. Hamilton's remark that a state has a much stronger duty than an individual to make its own welfare the guide of its actions conveys this view. Jefferson, however, tended to reject this distinction and held both to a uniform standard. In his view the moral law of our nature holds that the moral duties which exist between individuals in a state of nature

> accompany them into a state of society and the aggregate of the duties of all the individuals composing the society constitutes the duties of that society towards any other; so that between society and society the same moral duties exist as did between the individuals composing them while in an unassociated state, their maker not having released them from those duties on their forming themselves into a nation. Compacts then between nation and nation are obligatory on them by the same moral law which obliges individuals to observe their compacts.

If observing compacts constituted an important part of morality in international relations, Jefferson saw the British as especially immoral. "Why ally with faithless immoral England?" he asked John Langdon; England had "never admitted a chapter of morality" into her political practice.[20]

Finally, Jefferson returned to the similarity in forms of government and the hope of establishing republican governments elsewhere as a reason to be careful of appearing to side against France. What was the danger in not suspending the treaties? he asked. If it was the fear of being allied with a despotism, then it must be said that the alliance had been made with one in 1778. If the danger was in the possibility that France might become a republic, that was the hope of "the great mass of our constituents." The only part of the treaties which Jefferson thought could really lead to danger was the clause guaranteeing

19. "Opinion on the French Treaties," in Ford (ed.), *Jefferson Works*, VII, 295–98.
20. *Ibid.*, 285–86; Jefferson to Langdon, March 5, 1810, in Lipscomb and Bergh (eds.), *The Writings of Thomas Jefferson*, XIII, 373–79.

French possession of their West Indies. This part, he conceded, might have to be suspended, but, citing Vattel, in that case the United States would be bound to make compensation. To abrogate the treaty or refuse compensation would be to give France just cause for war against the United States. He maintained in the cabinet several months later, "I would not gratify the combination of kings with the spectacle of the two only republics on earth destroying each other for two cannon; nor would I, for infinitely greater cause, add this country to that combination, turn the scale of contests, and let it be from our hands that the hopes of man receive their last stab." [21]

As Helvidius, Madison also sought to link the cause of the French revolutionaries with that of the Americans. He did not subject the nature of the French cause to the more thorough analysis of Hamilton, but appeared to accept French declarations that their cause was liberty. Madison did not address himself at all to Hamilton's charges that the French did not deserve support because they had violated treaties, threatened all the crowned heads of Europe, initiated war, and conducted themselves badly; he seemed to assume that all wars for the cause of republicanism or liberty are inherently just. Again this made the internal regime criterion normative for the formation of American foreign policy.

The difficulty with this assumption is the extent to which such wars have an unlimited dimension. In that sense the American Revolution was the precursor of the French; yet, as Martin Clancy shows in his discussion of the conduct of the American Revolution, the Americans took pains to make their conduct of war conform to contemporary *jus in bello* standards. Edmund Burke's defense of the American Revolution and criticism of the French also suggests that the American war, though somewhat different from the European norm, still conformed to the just-war/limited-war tradition of the eighteenth century. [22]

21. "Opinion on the French Treaties" and "Reasons for his dissent in the *Little Sarah* case," in Ford (ed.), *Jefferson Works*, VII, 288–98 and 442.
22. Martin Clancy, "Rules of Land Warfare During the War of the American Revolution," 203–317; Friedrich von Gentz, "The French and American Revolutions Compared," *Three Revolutions*, trans. John Quincy Adams (Chicago, 1959), 52–63.

Madison's ultimate justification for identifying the French and American causes rested in his reading of popular sentiment. In his first letter Helvidius said that Pacificus was read with pleasure "by degenerate citizens among us, who hate our republican government, and the French revolution." In a private letter to Archibald Stuart, Madison reiterated his conviction that the people were attached to the Constitution, to the president, and to the French nation and revolution, while being averse to war, monarchy, and a political connection with Britain.

To Jefferson he wrote that the proclamation was being exploited by a pro-British commerce-oriented and "stockjobbing" minority, and he suggested the need to collect the genuine sense of the people or what he termed "the principles and sensations of the Agricultural which is the commanding part of the Society." [23]

Whether these represented the genuine sense of the people because they were the sentiments of a majority or because they were the sentiments of an *agricultural* majority Madison did not make clear. While Madison's own views on the superior virtue of farmers were ambiguous, Jefferson's were not. He regarded agriculture as a peculiarly moral occupation and particularly productive of civic virtue. Jefferson believed that "men are disposed to live honestly, if the means of doing so are open to them," and he firmly maintained that husbandry in a free-trade regime provided the means. If Jeffersonians were pessimistic about human nature when granted political power, they were optimistic about human nature when granted farmland. These two views were reconciled—by Jefferson at least—in a Rousseauean environmentalism which held that men are not naturally corrupt, lazy, or avaricious and become so only when special privilege exalts the few and depresses the many. Industry and commerce, like political power, promoted inequality and corruption and should be kept subservient to agriculture. It followed from this that the sentiments

---

23. "Helvidius, No. 1," and Madison to Stuart, September 1, 1793, in Hunt (ed.), *Madison Writings*, VI, 139 and 189–90; Madison to Jefferson, June 30, 1789, in Hutchinson *et al.* (eds.), *Madison Papers*, XII, 269; Madison to Jefferson, September 2, 1793, in Hunt (ed.), *Madison Writings*, VI, 191–93.

and principles of American farmers were the most accurate reflection of the moral sense which was part of every human soul. It also followed that agriculture be protected and promoted as an explicit policy goal.[24]

The Balance of Power

In his letters to Madison, Jefferson did not need to mention that the broad construction of the neutrality proclamation worked against their efforts to exploit the French-British rivalry. Helvidius complained that the proclamation was impolitic as well as unfair and unkind because it foreclosed the possibility of expanding ties with France, thereby forgoing "important advantages which [the United States] already enjoys, and those more important ones which it anxiously contemplates." As well-educated men familiar with diplomacy, Jefferson and Madison understood the workings of the balance of power principle and proved willing to use it to advance their conception of the common good. Madison in the Constitutional Convention had credited the balance of power, which made France and Britain rivals, for the success of the American revolution. During the Nootka Sound crisis in 1790, Jefferson had informed Gouverneur Morris in England that "a due balance on our borders is not less desirable to us, than a balance of power in Europe has always appeared to them."[25] Jefferson usually saw France as the best counterweight to the British; in 1803, however, when it appeared that Napoleon wished to reestablish a French empire in the Western Hemisphere based in Louisiana, Jefferson threatened to make an alliance with the

24. Jefferson to Madison, December 20, 1787, and Jefferson to William S. Smith, November 13, 1787, in Boyd *et al.* (eds.), *Jefferson Papers*, XII, 438–42. For a view which emphasizes Jefferson's flexibility on this question see Thomas Cragen, "Thomas Jefferson's Early Attitudes Toward Manufacturing, Agriculture, and Commerce" (Ph.D. dissertation, University of Tennessee, 1965), but more persuasive is Drew McCoy, *The Elusive Republic* (Chapel Hill, 1981). Other helpful discussions are Morton Frisch, "Hamilton's Report on Manufactures and Political Philosophy," *Publius*, VIII (Summer 1978), 129–34, and Joyce Appleby, "What Is Still American in the Political Philosophy of Thomas Jefferson?" *William and Mary Quarterly*, 3d ser., XXXIX (April, 1982), 287–309.

25. "Helvidius, No. 5," in Hunt (ed.), *Madison Writings*, V, 185; Jefferson to Morris, August 12, 1790, in Boyd *et al.* (eds.), *Jefferson Papers*, XVII, 127.

British. This, as the historian Henry Adams reports gleefully, went further than the supposed Anglophile Federalists had ever contemplated going. Two years later when he had set his sights on Spanish-owned Florida, Jefferson again suggested that the United States might make an alliance with Britain.[26]

Nevertheless, he implicitly distinguished the balance of power as a principle and as a system. While willing to exploit European rivalries which were part of the European system, Jefferson made it clear that he did not see the United States as part of that system. This helps to explain some of his sometimes cavalier dismissals of the importance of the European balance for American security. In 1810, for example, he wrote John Langdon that Federalist fears of being conquered by Bonaparte were "chimerical." Even if Napoleon incorporated Spain and Portugal into the French Empire, he would still have to subdue England and Russia; even if he succeeded in conquering England and Russia, he would look first to the East—Greece, Egypt, and India—as had Alexander the Great, his spiritual predecessor. Consequently, he argued, the United States had nothing to fear from Bonaparte and certainly should not "first let England plunder us, as she has been doing for years, for fear Bonaparte should do it."[27] By 1814 Jefferson returned to the view that American security depended on the maintenance of the balance system in Europe: "Surely none of us wish to see Bonaparte conquer Russia, and lay thus at his feet the whole continent of Europe. This done, England would be but a breakfast. . . . It cannot be to our interest that all Europe should be reduced to a single monarchy." Nevertheless, there were profound isolationist tendencies in Jeffersonianism, which preferred to occupy itself with the Western Hemisphere and ignore European affairs. Where Hamilton's design pointed to a time when the United States would take its place in a global system, Jefferson looked west and talked of "Chinese isolation."[28]

26. Adams, *History*, II, 135–50; Alfred Vagts, "The United States and the Balance of Power," *Journal of Politics*, III (November, 1941), 415–17.
27. Jefferson to Langdon, March 5, 1810, in Lipscomb and Bergh (eds.), *Jefferson Writings*, XII, 445.
28. Jefferson to Thomas Lieper, January 1, 1814, in Ford (ed.), *Jefferson Works*, IX, 445; Kaplan, "Jefferson, the Napoleonic Wars, and the Balance of Power," 204–10.

One way to confine Europeans to Europe was to insist upon a broad interpretation of American neutral rights. One of Jefferson's arguments in the cabinet against a proclamation had been that Washington ought to hold back a declaration of neutrality "as a thing worth something to the powers at war, that they would bid for it, and we might reasonably ask a price, the broadest privileges of neutral nations." Jeffersonian rhetoric on foreign policy rang with calls for free navigation, free trade, and nonimpressment, nonentanglement, and restricted definitions of contraband and blockade. The Model Treaty which the Continental Congress had established in preparation for the negotiations with France in 1778 had contained a very limited list of contraband goods, held that neutrals should have the right to trade with belligerents, and laid down the principle that free ships make free goods.[29]

Congress had based this treaty on the most liberal ones drawn up in Europe. Whatever reservations Jefferson had about individuals' participating in commercial activity did not prevent him from holding to free-trade principles. The reduction of British power, the expansion of neutral rights, and the freeing of international trade went together. He explained to Thomas Pinckney, United States minister to Great Britain, that the United States would follow the rights and duties of neutrality in its relations with Europe as marked out by the treaties that France had established with Holland and Britain in 1713. Where the treaties were silent, the United States would hold to the "modern" or "liberal" law of nations.

> The general principles of the law of nations must be the rule. I mean the principles of that law as they have been liberalized in latter times by the refinement of manners and morals, and evidenced by the Declarations, Stipulations, and Practice of every civilized nation. In our Treaty with Prussia, indeed, we have gone ahead of other Nations in doing away with

29. Jefferson to Madison, June 23, 1793, in Ford (ed.), *Jefferson Works*, VII, 407–08; Gilbert, *The Beginnings of American Foreign Policy*, 50–51; John Holladay Latane, "Jefferson's Influence on American Foreign Policy," *University of Virginia Alumni Bulletin*, 3d ser., XVII (July–August, 1924), 245–69.

restraints on the commerce of peaceful nations, by declaring that nothing shall be contraband.[30]

Jefferson held these principles dear partly because the American farmer would be a major beneficiary, and, as suggested above, Jefferson saw those farmers playing a special role in the American republic. British inclusion of food as contraband in 1793, he argued, revealed the illiberality of the British government; more fundamentally, it violated a natural right to buy and sell food. While war allowed nations to abridge the right to exchange military supplies, food continued to be exempt. Jefferson's indignation on this point resembled Hamilton's indignation on the seizure of alien private property during peacetime; both perhaps realized that the nature of international relations meant that these rights would continue to be at risk.[31]

Jeffersonian adherence to broad neutral principles linked the United States with other neutrals who also sought freedom of the seas, particularly Denmark and Sweden. The Armed Neutrality of 1780 had helped to isolate Britain during the American Revolutionary War and some looked to repeat that. Napoleon, for one, would loudly proclaim his commitment to "freedom of the seas," in seeking to create a continental alliance against British maritime preeminence. Some Jeffersonians toyed with the notion of joining such a league and Secretary of State Randolph's instructions to John Jay included the suggestion that Jay use the threat of joining to wrest concessions from the British. Hamilton, however, had already assured the British that the United States would do no such thing and it is doubtful that the idea was more than a threat. Nonentanglement with European powers was perhaps even more deeply engrained than adherence to broad neutral principles.[32]

30. Jefferson to Pinckney, May 7, 1793, in Ford (ed.), *Jefferson Works*, VII, 314–15.
31. Jefferson to Pinckney, September 7, 1793, in Lipscomb and Bergh (eds.), *Jefferson Writings*, IX, 220–27.
32. McDonald, *The Presidency of George Washington*, 143; DeConde, *The Quasi-War*, 294–312; Jefferson to Paine, March 18, 1801, in Ford (ed.), *Jefferson Works*, VIII, 8.

National Power

Contrary to what is sometimes asserted about Jefferson, he did concern himself with the means of foreign policy and not simply with abstract ideals. As suggested above, he understood and attempted to use the balance of power principle; if he rarely seemed comfortable with the military components such a principle might entail it was partly from a fear of the consequences of standing armies and partly because he regarded American trade and primary products as the country's most potent weapons in diplomacy. As he wrote to Thomas Pinckney in 1797, "War is not the best engine for us to resort to, nature has given us one in our commerce."[33]

Vattel had sanctioned commercial measures as one way to oppose a rising power. Force of arms was not the only means available to guard against a formidable power; alliances, confederations, and discriminatory trading policies could also be used to augment one's own strength and diminish that of a large power. Hamilton had also advocated "prohibitory regulations" as one way for the nation to advance its welfare, in *Federalist* Number 11. An important advantage of the strong national government envisioned in the Constitution would be its ability to do just that. Hamilton did not stop with this, however, and he went on to discuss the importance of establishing a federal navy powerful enough to throw its weight into the scale of two contending powers. He also made numerous proposals throughout the 1790s to strengthen and professionalize the army. Additionally his financial measures must be seen as efforts to multiply the means available to American statesmen in the future. Jefferson, on the other hand, tended to rely almost exclusively on commercial policy, a strategy of "peaceable coercion," which critics derided as one in which either side counted upon exhausting its opponent by injuring itself.[34]

Jefferson first noted the possibility of war between France and Britain in a letter to Madison in March 1793. This meant that the maritime powers (Holland and Great Britain) would probably combine to disrupt French commerce, which would mean stopping the

33. Jefferson to Pinckney, May 29, 1797, in Ford (ed.), *Jefferson Works*, VII, 493.
34. Vattel, Book III, Chap. 3, sec. 46; Hamilton, Jay, and Madison, *The Federalist Papers*, 85–87; Adams, *History*, II, 145.

flow of American goods to France. This, Jefferson claimed, would constitute a justifiable cause for war, but he thought that instead of declaring war against the maritime powers, a strategy of nonimportation ought to be followed. Such a course would "furnish us a happy opportunity of setting another example to the world by showing that nations may be brought to justice by appeals to their interests as well as by appeals to arms."[35] Appealing to interest understood as an appeal to material comfort was something which Jefferson believed that the United States with its great natural resources was in an excellent position to provide.

Madison shared Jefferson's faith in the strength of the American economy and thus in the efficacy of using commercial regulations to influence the behavior of other states. They both also insisted on sequestration as a right and as a weapon available for use by a power which lacked military means to advance its foreign policy. In 1790 and again in 1794 Madison worked hard in Congress to pass measures of commercial discrimination against British shipping. Discrimination, he argued, would encourage the development of American shipping (close to Madison's heart but rare in a southerner), would force the British to grant the United States reciprocity in commerce, and would lessen the reliance of American commerce on British credits and markets. Finally, Madison also employed an argument from justice or nature; the extent of British commerce, he claimed, was "unnatural" because too much American produce went to the British.

To objections that these measures would harm the American economy more than the British, Madison replied that the American situation was more advantageous because it exported chiefly the "necessaries" of life: the raw materials on which the more industrialized economies of Europe relied. It would be easier for the United States to replace lost finished goods (or get along without them) than for the British to replace the primary products provided by the United States. In making what now sounds like a peculiar argument, Madison explicitly drew on the country-city or farmer-merchant imagery noted above.

35. Jefferson to Madison, March, 1793, in Ford (ed.), *Jefferson Works*, VII, 250.

What we receive from other nations are but luxuries to us, which, if we choose to throw aside, we could deprive part of the manufacturers of those luxuries, of even bread, if we are forced, to the contest of self-denial. This being the case, our country may make her enemies feel the extent of her power. We stand, with respect to the nation exporting those luxuries, in the relation of an opulent individual to the laborer, in producing the superfluities for his accommodation; the former can do without these luxuries, the consumption of which gives bread to the latter.

For Madison Great Britain was doubly dependent on the United States: her West Indies could not subsist without American supplies, especially American grain and lumber, and her manufacturers could not subsist without American customers.[36]

To suggestions that such threats would provoke Great Britain to make war on the United States Madison replied that he refused to believe that the British would want to make war on a country which was the best market she had for her industrial goods, which provided an annual balance of ten or twelve million dollars in specie, and which provided supplies essential to the West Indies, the vital link for the British imperial economy. American granaries fed the West Indies; remove them and the entire British system would be threatened. The various nonintercourse and embargo bills that the Jeffersonians sponsored and enacted reflected this understanding. Thus in 1807 Jefferson thought or hoped that an embargo would protect American property from the belligerents by removing it from the seas, would force the belligerents to revoke their decrees, would strike a blow for neutral rights, and perhaps even help to win the Floridas from Spain.[37]

Madison held similar views during his presidency. J. C. A. Stagg has argued that Madison finally decided to invade Canada during the War of 1812 not as an object of territorial acquisition but in order to enforce a more effective embargo against the imperial system. Contrary to his earlier view of the uselessness of Canada to that system,

36. Drew McCoy, "Republicanism and American Foreign Policy: James Madison and the Political Economy of Commercial Discrimination," *William and Mary Quarterly*, 3d ser., XXI (October, 1974), 634–36; Speech of January 3, 1794, in Hunt (ed.), *Madison Writings*, VI, 207; Madison to Jefferson, June 30, 1787, in Hutchinson *et al.*, (eds.), *Madison Papers*, XII, 268–69.
37. Kaplan, "Jefferson, the Napoleonic Wars, and the Balance of Power," 201.

Madison came to realize that Canada was performing the role once played by the United States. In order to make the West Indies suffer, Madison had to try to close off the Canadian connection. Unfortunately the vaunted militia failed utterly as an effective military force, with the notable exception of the forces under the command of General Andrew Jackson.[38]

Interest and Ambition

The use of avarice to counter ambition, which is implicit in Jefferson's appeal to "interest" as opposed to an appeal to arms and in Madison's proposal to require those who desire war to pay for it ("Were a nation to impose such restraints on itself, avarice would be sure to calculate the expenses of ambition"), drew on a distinction and opposition made between "passions" and "interests" common in eighteenth-century discourse. Albert O. Hirschman in his study on the subject shows that the early modern political philosophers, having dethroned "visionary" premodern political philosophy, which taught (without offering much guaranty of success) the subordination of the passions to the higher faculties, that is, reason or devotion, sought to tame what they had liberated. This they thought could be done by using one set of passions to counter and check others. In particular these philosophers suggested that those passions "hitherto known variously as greed, avarice, or love of lucre, could be usefully employed to oppose and bridle such other passions as ambition, lust for power, or sexual lust." They emphasized the utility of the former passions by redefining them neutrally as "interests." The connection this word already had with money and banking contributed to this shift. "Interest," as in Jefferson's usage, meant concern for one's material well-being and comfort, a concern which the thinkers of the Enlightenment contrasted favorably with religious zeal or aristocratic pursuit of illusory glory. Enlightenment thinkers characterized the passions as unpredictable and destructive, the interests as

38. J. C. A. Stagg, "James Madison and the Coercion of Great Britain; Canada, the West Indies, and the War of 1812," *William and Mary Quarterly*, 3d ser., XXXVIII (January, 1981), 3–34; Theodore Roosevelt, *Gouverneur Morris* (Boston, 1895), 303–304.

predictable, constant, and mundane. In an age which rejected religious zealotry and which featured the rise of the middle classes, a redirection of human efforts toward material security promised stability in international as well as domestic politics. Unlike ambition, which was viewed as a passion of the few, avarice was, in the words of David Hume, "a universal passion which operates at all times in all places and upon all persons."[39]

On the strength of this understanding, Montesquieu argued that commerce was a peaceful and civilizing activity and that commercial republics were pacific in nature. David Hume also stressed that civilizing nature of commerce which brought people together, acquainted them with the taste for delicacy and luxury, and encouraged industry. The more refined arts advanced, the more sociable men became.[40]

Not everyone who accepted this distinction was so optimistic that interest would check passion. John Quincy Adams, commenting on Jefferson's policy of "peaceable coercion," wrote that "a reliance upon the operation of measures, from their effect on the interests, however clear and unequivocal, of nations, cannot be safe against a counter current of their passions." Nations, like individuals, would sometimes sacrifice their peace to pride, hatred, envy, jealousy, mistaken policy, or national madness. France, for the Federalists, exemplified the sacrifice of interest to ambition. Fisher Ames frequently compared France to Rome, because he thought both embodied a passion for conquest which overruled the careful calculations of a country like commercial England: "The avarice of a commercial nation calculates the means and reckons up the value of them; a conquering nation disdains both gold and arithmetic."[41]

Hamilton in *Federalist* Number 6 had forcefully expressed his doubts about the peaceableness of commercial republics. The private passions of political men "whether the favorites of a king or of a people" had often led them to sacrifice the public good. More than

39. Albert O. Hirschman, *The Passions and the Interests* (Princeton, 1977), 25–54; Hume, in Green and Grose (eds.), *Philosophical Works*, III, 176.
40. Hirschman, *The Passions and the Interests*, 60–64; Hume, in Green and Grose (eds.), *Philosophical Works*, II, 35.
41. John Quincy Adams, *Lives of Madison and Monroe* (Buffalo, 1850), 88; "Phocion, No. 6," in Ames (ed.), *Works of Fisher Ames*, II, 170.

that, however, he saw that commerce would become another incentive for war and not its pacifier: "Have there not been as many wars founded on commercial motives since that has become the prevailing system of nations, as were before occasioned by the cupidity of territory or dominion?" Like Adams, Hamilton doubted that the "rationality" of avarice (or "interest") could often overcome the stronger passions of ambition, the desire for preeminence, and the love of rule. He would not let his readers forget that men—even commercial men—are "ambitious, vindictive, and rapacious." Finally Hamilton doubted that the people were any more prone to peace than kings. His review of history suggested to him that there had been almost as many popular as royal wars. While this did not reduce his commitment to republican government, it certainly reduced his willingness to make the internal composition of other states a primary foreign-policy consideration.[42]

The Jay Treaty

Jeffersonians, in opposing the Jay Treaty, relied precisely on England's "calculating" character. Where Hamilton feared that retaliatory commercial measures would act on British pride—and bring on war, Madison asked, "Was it conceivable that Great Britain, with all the dangers and embarrassments which are threatening upon her, would wantonly make war on a country which was the best market in the world?" The ratification of the treaty postponed the experiment which might have answered this question, and the Jeffersonians would have to wait until the embargo of 1807–1808 and the War of 1812 to discover that it was conceivable.[43]

Because Jeffersonians had a higher estimate of American strength than the Federalists did, they maintained that the United States ought to have held out for more comprehensive goals than the treaty provided. They complained that the treaty lacked reciprocity and gave up too much to the British, particularly on the issues of broad neutral rights which they considered of vital interest. Albert Gallatin

42. Hamilton, Jay, and Madison, *The Federalist Papers*, 54–58.
43. Speech of April 6, 1796, in Hunt (ed.), *Madison Writings*, VI, 295; Stagg, "James Madison and the Coercion of Great Britain," 20–34.

argued that more should have been said in the treaty about contraband, blockades, the free-ships-make-free-goods principle, impressment, and British spoliations of American commerce. These would remain American demands as long as war raged in Europe. Jefferson even rejected a treaty with the British, negotiated by Monroe in 1806, on the grounds that it did not adequately treat the problem of impressment.

By acquiescing in the British interpretation of neutrality, the Americans had effectively made themselves allies of the British; by limiting the ability of the United States to restrict British trade and sequester British debts, the treaty deprived the United States of its most effective weapons. Since Madison, Gallatin, and the other republicans did not believe that American rejection of the treaty would lead to war—as the Federalists argued—they regarded these concessions as completely unnecessary. From their stronghold in the House of Representatives, these republicans sought to invoke the appropriation power to prevent the execution of the Jay Treaty. Once again, as in the debate over the Proclamation of Neutrality, a foreign policy question developed into a constitutional issue, this time with the House of Representatives asserting a right to give its consent to treaties. A constitutional crisis was averted, however, when the House narrowly approved legislation to fund the treaty.[44]

Approval of the Jay Treaty soured relations with France and led to the undeclared war between France and the United States during John Adams' tenure as president and Jefferson's as vice-president. The French and some of their American supporters justified their plunder of American commerce as just reprisal and as indemnity for American abandonment of the principle of free ships, free goods which had been embodied in the 1778 treaties between France and the United States. Jeffersonians regarded the quasi war as a tragic mistake; to Jefferson the natural affection which bound the two nations together had been brought "by the ill temper of their executive administra-

44. House Debate on the Jay Treaty, April 26, 1796, in E. James Ferguson (ed.), *Selected Writings of Albert Gallatin* (New York, 1967), 96–102; Speech of April 6, 1796, in Hunt (ed.), *Madison Writings*, VI, 278–88; Henkin, *Foreign Affairs and the Constitution*, 148–51.

tions" to the brink of war. The quasi war confirmed once again the peculiar penchant of the executive branch of any government to entertain thoughts of war.[45]

Jeffersonians dismissed the threat of a French invasion as a hoax and argued that the Federalists invented the threat to subdue internal adversaries and to subvert republican government. Under the Federalists the government was in the hands of a "monarchical aristocratical party" whose object was to make over the American constitution after the British model. The Hamiltonian financial system, the expansive claims of executive power, the creation of standing armies, the creation of a large public debt, and the cultivation of close ties with Great Britain were all pursued with this end in mind. Jeffersonian accusations gained new credibility with the passage of the Alien and Sedition Acts, which, as an effort to muzzle political opposition, backfired and contributed significantly to the Federalist defeat in 1800.[46]

By concentrating on the domestic consequences of the military buildup which the Federalists advocated, the Jeffersonians again looked to the detachment of the United States from the European balance, and they downplayed the significance of the European balance for American security. As Albert Gallatin argued, Europe was not America's concern:

> But however interesting that balance may be to Europe, how does it concern us? We may lament the fate of Poland and Venice, and I never can myself see, without regret, independent nations blotted from the map of the world. But their destiny does not affect us in the least. We have no interest whatsoever in that balance, and by us it should be altogether forgotten and neglected. If we ever think we have an interest in it, shall we not be induced to throw our weight in the scale; shall we not involve ourselves in the destinies and wars of Europe?[47]

45. Jefferson to Burr, June 17, 1797, in Lipscomb and Bergh (eds.), *Jefferson Writings*, IX, 404; Madison to Jefferson, April 2, 1798, in Hunt (ed.), *Madison Writings*, VI, 312.
46. DeConde, *The Quasi-War*, 192–96.
47. House Debate on the Foreign Intercourse Bill, in Ferguson (ed.), *Writings of Albert Gallatin*, 127.

Summary

Thus, in spite of Hamilton's efforts (and to a certain extent because of them), the Jeffersonian public philosophy replaced the Federalists'. We may now draw some tentative conclusions about how the new consensus affected the American interpretation of the just-war/limited-war tradition.

1. Jeffersonians defined the American national interest more broadly than the Federalists. Neutral rights, free trade, and republicanism may be described as what Arnold Wolfers calls "milieu goals." Nations pursuing such goals "are not out to defend or increase possessions they hold to the exclusion of others, but aim instead at shaping conditions beyond their national boundaries."[48] Jeffersonians rightly claimed that their goals served American interests, but they could also plausibly maintain that other nations would benefit as well. If the British could be forced to change their practice on neutral rights and on trade, all the neutral nations, including the United States, would be better off. But while the Jeffersonians knew what kind of milieu they wanted, they did not think enough about how they would achieve it. To the extent that their efforts undermined or ignored the European balance, they made it less likely that the milieu they desired would come into being.

2. Jeffersonians made the nature of other countries' regimes one criterion in making foreign policy or in considering the resort to force. When Henry Clay demanded that the United States government take a stand against monarchist Spain by supporting the independence of the Latin American revolutionaries or again by supporting the Greek revolutionaries, he employed the same sort of criterion. Other Jeffersonians, like Albert Gallatin, took the view that the United States ought to be the "model republic" whose example would bring hope to oppressed people in other lands, but which would do no more than that.[49]

3. Jeffersonians also made the domestic consequences to the

48. Arnold Wolfers, *Discord and Collaboration* (Baltimore, 1962), 74.
49. "Examination of the Mexican War," in Ferguson (ed.), *Writings of Albert Gallatin*, 343.

United States of a resort to force an important criterion in public debate. Again and again Americans have asked themselves about the effect of a war or some other foreign policy action upon the institutional balance established in the Constitution, upon the character of the American people, and upon the American self-perception as transmitters of certain ideals. Jeffersonians counted as harmful consequences ones which Hamilton regarded as beneficial (growth of a commercial class, promotion of manufactures, energetic executive), but both saw foreign policy as a way to advance domestic political goals. In this respect revisionist historians, who emphasize the way American foreign policy has advanced commercial values or preserved the "military-industrial complex," write in a venerable American tradition.

4. Jeffersonian constitutional doctrines, which emphasized legislative dominance and suspicion of the executive, helped push the *jus ad bellum* to the point where only wars of self-defense were sanctioned. This trend had been a tendency in Vattel's teaching—just war based on injury—but was exacerbated by the fear of executive power and the possibility of diplomatic wars initiated by that branch. Where the maintenance of the balance of power or justice itself might require offensive war, the Jeffersonian doctrine stood in the way. Such actions did not disappear, of course, but reemerged in an expanded and sometimes ludicrous notion of self-defense. Thus James Polk justified his actions against Mexico by saying that the Mexicans had attacked first. This led to Abraham Lincoln's famous "spot" resolutions which asked to be shown the very spot where the Mexican army had attacked the American army; memory of this may have led to Lincoln's efforts to have the South fire the first shot at Fort Sumter. It is also in appreciation of this fact that President Franklin D. Roosevelt is sometimes accused of having "set up" the attack on Pearl Harbor.

5. Jeffersonian commitment to the militia rather than a professional army tended to blur *jus in bello* distinctions which made sense of rules of noncombatancy. If all citizens were potential or actual soldiers, the rules would be harder to apply and might pass into irrelevance. When combined with Napoleonic strategies of "annihilation" rather than "attrition," this commitment had the further effect of to-

talizing war and engaging popular passions in a more direct way than the just-war tradition had envisioned.[50]

6. Jeffersonians saw themselves as acting in the spirit of the just-war/limited-war tradition when they chose economic measures over the use of military force. Commercial retaliation represented another way for a nation to register the seriousness of its grievances short of war, and thereby provided more flexibility for statesmen by giving them another power lever short of resorting to force.

7. The Jeffersonian understanding of human nature as easily malleable by social and economic conditions raised extravagant hopes about the possibilities of reforming human beings by reforming their governments and social institutions. Whereas the just-war/limited-war tradition assumed that warring was bound up in human nature so that the problem was not to eliminate but to limit war, the Jeffersonian understanding suggested that, given the right environment, such elimination might be possible.

50. Russell Weigley, *The American Way of War* (New York, 1973).

CHAPTER VI

Conclusion

The Congress of Vienna reestablished a balance of power system in Europe, ushered in a period of relative peace and stability, and reimposed monarchical principles of legitimacy on the Continent. The European nations had coalesced, albeit belatedly, to turn back the new threat of universal monarchy posed by Napoleonic France; European statesmen had restored the intellectual and structural framework which made possible the operation of a moderate balance of power system; and with sovereigns once again committed to moderate aims, agreements to govern the conduct of war could and would be made. In all these respects the Concert of Europe vindicated the Vattelian conception of international politics and law, making apt Vollenhoven's characterization of this period as the "Age of Vattel."

The justice of the war pursued by the final coalition against France could be established by referring to the injury to the independence of the European states and to the overthrow of the European balance by the French. Vattel's work sanctioned both of these causes and both appeared in the statements of general war aims made by the leading statesmen of the coalition, Britain's Castlereagh and Austria's Metternich. Thus Metternich defined Austria's ultimate objective in joining the Allies "as a great voluntary . . . alliance in the center of Europe, based on the independence of states and the security of property which would found a system of justice to replace the existing system of forced coalitions . . . and to oppose any designs for aggrandisement, from whatever quarter."[1]

These references to justice did not lead Metternich or Castlereagh to advocate either total war or total victory; their war aims remained distinctly and emphatically limited. They both assumed that they had to work within a system of sovereign states and neither made the domestic structure of France the object of the war. In November 1813, for example, Metternich declared that Napoleon could have peace on the basis of the natural frontiers of France; if Napoleon had accepted, he would have retained the leadership of the territories of historic France and would also have secured for his son the right of succession to the imperial French throne. It was not in Napoleon's character, however, to accept others' terms, no matter how moderate; yet the peace terms underscored Metternich's insistence that the war was not directed against France, but against French predominance. Looking beyond the immediate problem of defeating France, Metternich and the Allies realized that the reestablishment of a stable equilibrium required a continued role for France. Thus, in Henry Kissinger's words: "The Allies wished to see France great and powerful, . . . but they also desired a peaceful existence for themselves and would not rest until they had achieved a just equilibrium of power."[2]

Accordingly, when Napoleon had been defeated and exiled, the Allies resisted the temptation of a punitive peace. In spite of popular resentments and the desire for vengeance, the Allies made a remarkably generous peace with France. This brought France back into the system without nurturing a sense of injustice which might have made France anxious to overturn the system. In addition, as Gulick notes, the Allies did not make the Bourbons, who replaced Napoleon, the heirs of their hostility toward Napoleon. This followed logically from the Metternichian emphasis on legitimacy and from the definition of war aims as the reduction of French preponderance rather than as the reordering of the French regime. Intentionally or not, this also conformed to Vattel's dictum that the sovereign and not the nation ought

1. Henry Kissinger, *A World Restored: Metternich, Castlereagh, and the Problems of Peace*, 1812–22 (Boston, 1957), 51.
2. *Ibid.*, 103; Gulick, *Europe's Classical Balance of Power*, 148–49.

to bear the burden of punishment for conducting an unjust war. For Vattel, justice and moderation went hand in hand.[3]

The peace brought on by the Concert of Europe also vindicated Hamilton's analysis and approach. The Jeffersonians had worried about the consequences of a French defeat for American republicanism virtually from the outbreak of war in 1793. That year Jefferson wrote his friend Harry Innes:

> It is very necessary for us then to keep clear of the European combustion, if they will let us. This they will do probably if France is successful but if great successes were to attend the arms of the kings, it is far from certain they might not chuse [*sic*] to finish their job completely, by obliging us to change in the form of our government at least.

Jeffersonian assertions of the indivisibility of French and American liberty came out of this concern, against which Hamilton had argued that the rivalry of the European monarchs would make American liberty secure. With Britain victorious in 1814, the Jeffersonians fully expected a British assault on the United States, but it never came, for reasons which Hamilton had suggested. "The consideration of the unsatisfactory state of the negotiations at Vienna," "the alarming situation of the interior of France," and "the state of [British] finances" made the British want to bring the American war to a quick conclusion. So the British made their peace with the United States and restored the status quo ante bellum with the Treaty of Ghent.[4]

On the other hand, the peace did not sustain the American or broad neutralist interpretation of the law of nations. The British continued to regard their definition of maritime rights as a vital interest; they considered the right to blockade and the right to search neutral vessels the major factors in ending Napoleon's domination. The Americans, who had made no significant gains in their war against the British, were in no position to alter the British stand on these points. Thus the negotiations between the Americans and the British left unsettled the issues of freedom of the seas, broad neutral rights, and impressment. Hamilton had been correct in seeing how vital the

---

3. Gulick, *Europe's Classical Balance of Power*, 178.
4. Jefferson to Innes, May 23, 1793, in Ford (ed.), *Jefferson Works*, VII, 343; Bemis, *John Quincy Adams*, 217.

British considered maritime rights to be for their well-being, in believing that the United States lacked the power to establish broad neutral rights, and in assuming that such rights would be difficult to sustain in wartime anyway.

Agreement on other issues, however, allowed the British to turn to European affairs undisturbed by the prospect of trouble with the United States. This made possible a convergence of interests between the United States and Great Britain which Hamilton had hinted at in his Nootka Sound opinion and in his correspondence with Rufus King during the quasi war with France. Protected by the British navy and open to the flow of British capital, the United States would steadily grow to become the hemispheric power which Hamilton had envisioned; assured of American trade and of the exclusion of the continental powers from the Western Hemisphere, Great Britain would be able to resume its traditional policy of "splendid isolation" and of holding the European balance. By 1823 the Americans could act more independently than Hamilton had been able to do. Samuel F. Bemis rightly emphasizes that the courses the United States and Britain pursued involved separate and parallel rather than joint action or a "temporary alliance" of the sort that Hamilton had contemplated. That the United States was able to strike out on a more independent course reflected in part the growing strength of the young republic which Hamilton had labored so hard to promote.[5]

Ironically, this state of affairs also appeared to confirm the Jeffersonian insistence on the superiority of republican governments' foreign policies and on the separation of the United States from the European balance. Republican institutions had proved themselves resistant to war, particularly offensive war; the Americans had sought to limit the effects of war even more than Vattel envisioned by defending broad neutral rights; and American diplomacy had fostered pacific settlement of disputes. Indeed, the Claims Commissions established by the Jay Treaty gave impetus to the revival of the judicial process of international arbitration which had been used frequently during medieval times, but which had fallen into disuse during the eighteenth century. These commissions were widely imitated and set

5. Bemis, *John Quincy Adams*, 397–403.

a precedent for the submission of the claims of Great Britain and the United States over the *Alabama* case to arbitration following the Civil War, which in turn served as the model for the arbitration processes institutionalized in the Hague conventions of 1899 and 1907.[6]

Americans throughout the nineteenth century tended to attribute these advances to the superiority of American principles and institutions, blissfully ignoring how essential the European equilibrium (and British naval dominance) was to American success. Jefferson reverted to the condemnation of the balance of power when, at the time when the Monroe Doctrine was being shaped, he wrote President Monroe:

> I have ever deemed it fundamental for the United States never to take active part in the quarrels of Europe. Their political interests are entirely distinct from ours. Their mutual jealousies, their balance of power, their complicated alliances, their forms and principles of government, are all foreign to us. They are nations of eternal war. All their energies are expended in the destruction of the labor, property and lives of their people. On our part, never had a people so favorable a chance of trying to oppose systems of peace and fraternity with mankind, and the direction of all our means and faculties to the purposes of improvement instead of destruction.[7]

The peace established at Vienna was not perfect, as no human contrivance is. Parts of the settlement plainly contradicted the law of nations, and the maneuvering of the diplomats in restoring a balance of power system were by no means simply altruistic in character, since each sought to maintain and enhance his principal's territory and power. Use of the means of compensation for the sake of a more stable equilibrium sometimes required the destruction of smaller sovereignties; the establishment of spheres of influence required the attenuation of the sovereignty of others; and the Continental Great Powers insisted on their right to intervene in the affairs of smaller countries on behalf of monarchical legitimacy. Each of these weak-

6. Brierly, *Law of Nations*, 348–50.
7. Vagts, "The United States and the Balance of Power," 416–19; DeConde, *The Quasi-War*, 336; Jefferson to Monroe, June 11, 1823, in Ford (ed.), *Jefferson Works*, X, 257.

ened the claim that the balance of power system preserved the independence of states, a prime concern of international law.

On the other hand, Vattel had suggested that sovereignties which were unable to defend themselves were imperfect, and he offered an elastic conception of sovereignty which permitted states within the orbit of a larger state to consider themselves still sovereign. Ultimately, Vattelians argued, a balance of power system presented perhaps the only guaranty of the public law of Europe. Additionally, the Congress of Vienna provided the foundation for the Concert of Europe, the first continuing quasi-institutional structure of the European states system. The system of ad hoc conferences and congresses which met throughout the nineteenth century helped to foster a sense of the value of the system as a whole and made more evident the "republic of Europe" which Vattel had described a half-century earlier.[8]

Finally, this restoration of the European balance of power system did not completely defeat the new intellectual currents, sociological movements, and structural changes which the American and French revolutions had unleashed. Liberalism and nationalism reopened the question of right authority in favor of democratic or ethnic interpretations (wars of "national liberation") which made the European system only "semi-homogenous," as Raymond Aron put it. Thus Europe never achieved the same degree of moral consensus that could have more easily neutralized conflicts and supplied standards for common judgments and actions as existed in medieval or eighteenth-century Europe. Temptations for Britain or for members of the Holy Alliance to intervene in other countries in the name of liberalism or monarchical restoration accordingly persisted, coincident with continuing efforts to improve or preserve strategic position.

With the conclusion of the Napoleonic Wars the European balance of power system operated with and in an altered structural framework. It had consolidated its membership, yet found itself separated from the Western Hemisphere, with the British navy the uncontested mistress of the seas, and with Russia, uncertainly committed to equi-

8. Vagts and Vagts, "The Balance of Power in International Law," 565–67; F. H. Hinsley, *Power and the Pursuit of Peace* (Cambridge, 1963), 213–26.

librist principles, a European as well as an Asiatic power. These shifts anticipated the eclipse of the European system by a world system which would emerge with World War I. Those who sought to shape the new order rejected the link between the balance of power and international law; ironically, they were led by the United States, which had once relied so heavily on those who taught the importance of that linkage.[9]

9. Raymond Aron, *Peace and War: A Theory of International Relations*, trans. Richard Howard and Annette Baker Fox (Garden City, N.Y. 1966), 100–104; Morgenthau, *Politics Among Nations*, 442; Dehio, *The Precarious Balance*, 179.

Selected Bibliography

BOOKS

Ames, Seth, ed. *The Works of Fisher Ames*, 2 vols. New York, 1971.

Aron, Raymond. *Peace and War: A Theory of International Relations.* Translated by Richard Howard and Annette Baker Fox. Garden City, N.Y., 1966.

Bemis, Samuel F. *John Quincy Adams and the Foundations of American Foreign Policy.* New York, 1949.

Boyd, Julian, *et al.*, eds. *The Papers of Thomas Jefferson.* 20 vols. Princeton, 1950–

Brierly, J. L. *The Law of Nations.* Oxford, 1963.

Bull, Hedley. *The Anarchical Society.* New York, 1977.

Burt, A. L. *The United States, Great Britain, and British North America.* New Haven, 1940.

Butterfield, Herbert, and Martin Wight, eds. *Diplomatic Investigations.* London, 1966.

Claude, Inis L., Jr. *Power and International Relations.* New York, 1962.

Colbourn, Trevor, ed. *Fame and the Founding Fathers: Essays by Douglass Adair.* New York, 1974.

165

Dante. *On World Government*. Translated by Herbert Schneider. Indianapolis, 1957.

Davenant, Charles. *Essays Upon the Balance of Power, the Right of Making War, Peace, and Alliances, and Universal Monarchy*. London, 1701.

DeConde, Alexander. *Entangling Alliance: Politics and Diplomacy Under George Washington*. Durham, N.C., 1958.

―――. *The Quasi-War: The Politics and Diplomacy of the Undeclared War with France, 1797–1801*. New York, 1966.

Dehio, Ludwig. *The Precarious Balance*. Translated by Charles Fullman. New York, 1962.

Donelan, Michael, ed. *The Reason of States*. London, 1978.

Earle, Edward, ed. *Makers of Modern Strategy*. Princeton, 1952.

Farrand, Max, ed. *The Records of the Federal Convention*. 4 vols. New Haven, 1937.

Fitzpatrick, John, ed. *The Writings of George Washington*. 39 vols. Washington, D.C., 1931–44.

Ford, Paul L., ed. *The Works of Thomas Jefferson*. 12 vols. New York, 1905.

Ford, Worthington, ed. *The Papers of John Quincy Adams*. 7 vols. New York, 1913–17.

Forsyth, M. G., H. M. A. Keens-Soper, and P. Savigear, eds. *The Theory of International Relations*. London, 1970.

Gilbert, Felix. *The Beginnings of American Foreign Policy: To the Farewell Address*. New York, 1965.

Grotius, Hugo. *The Rights of War and Peace*. Translated by A. C. Campbell. Washington, D.C., 1901.

Gulick, Edward V. *Europe's Classical Balance of Power*. New York, 1955.

166

Hamilton, Alexander, John Jay, and James Madison. *The Federalist Papers*. New York, 1961.

Henkins, Louis. *Foreign Affairs and the Constitution*. New York, 1972.

Howard, Michael. *War in European History*. Oxford, 1976.

Hume, David. *Philosophical Works*. Edited by T. H. Green and T. H. Grose. Vol. II of 4 vols. Darmstadt, 1964.

Hunt, Gaillard, ed. *The Writings of James Madison*. 9 vols. New York, 1900–1910.

Hutchinson, William T., *et al.*, eds. *The Papers of James Madison*. 12 vols. Chicago, 1962–

Johnson, James T. *Ideology, Reason, and the Limitation of War*. Princeton, 1975.

———. *Just War Tradition and the Restraint of War*. Princeton, 1981.

Lipscomb, Andrew, and Albert Bergh, eds. *The Writings of Thomas Jefferson*. 20 vols. Washington, D.C., 1904–1905.

Lycan, Gilbert. *Alexander Hamilton and American Foreign Policy*. Norman, Okla., 1970.

Malone, Dumas. *Jefferson and the Rights of Man*. Boston, 1951.

McCloskey, Robert, ed. *The Works of James Wilson*. 2 vols. Cambridge, Mass., 1967.

McCoy, Drew. *The Elusive Republic*. Chapel Hill, 1981.

McDonald, Forrest. *The Presidency of George Washington*. New York, 1975.

Montesquieu. *Oeuvres Complètes*. Paris, 1964.

Morgenthau, Hans. *Politics Among Nations*. 5th ed. New York, 1973.

Osgood, Robert, and Robert W. Tucker. *Force, Order, and Justice*. Baltimore, 1967.

Richardson, James, ed. *A Compilation of the Messages and Papers of the Presidents*. 11 vols. Washington, D.C., 1911.

Roosevelt, Theodore. *Gouverneur Morris*. Boston, 1898.

Ruddy, F. S. *International Law in the Enlightenment. The Background of Emmerich de Vattel's "Le Droit des Gens."* Dobbs Ferry, N.Y., 1975.

Storing, Herbert. *What the Anti-Federalists Were For*. Chicago, 1981.

Stourzh, Gerald. *Alexander Hamilton and the Idea of Republican Government*. Stanford, 1970.

Stuart, Reginald. *The Half-Way Pacifist: Thomas Jefferson's View of War*. Toronto, 1978.

Syrett, Harold C., and Jacob Cooke, eds. *The Papers of Alexander Hamilton*. 26 vols. New York, 1963–79.

Vattel, Emmerich de. *The Law of Nations; or, Principles of the Law of Nature, Applied to the Conduct and Affairs of Nations and Sovereigns*. Translated by Joseph Chitty. 6th ed. Philadelphia, 1844.

Varg, Paul. *Foreign Policies of the Founding Fathers*. Baltimore, 1970.

Vincent, R. J. *Nonintervention and International Order*. Princeton, 1974.

Vollenhoven, Cornelius Van. *The Three Stages in the Evolution of the Law of Nations*. The Hague, 1919.

Walzer, Michael. *Just and Unjust Wars*. New York, 1977.

Wolf, John B. *Toward a European Balance of Power, 1620–1715*. Chicago, 1970.

Wolfers, Arnold. *Discord and Collaboration*. Baltimore, 1962.

Woolery, William K. *The Relation of Thomas Jefferson to American Foreign Policy*. Baltimore, 1927.

ARTICLES

Bowman, Alfred. "Jefferson, Hamilton, and American Foreign Policy." *Political Science Quarterly*, LXXI (March, 1956), 18–41.

Childress, James F. "Just-War Theories." *Theological Studies*, XXXIX (1978), 427–45.

Clancy, Martin. "Rules of Land Warfare During the War of the American Revolution." *Yearbook of World Polity*, II (1962), 203–317.

Claude, Inis L., Jr. "Just Wars: Doctrines and Institutions." *Political Science Quarterly*, XCV (Spring, 1980), 83–96.

Elbe, Joachim von. "The Evolution of the Concept of the Just War in International Law." *American Journal of International Law*, XXX (October, 1939), 665–88.

Fenwick, Charles G. "The Authority of Vattel." *American Political Science Review*, VII (August, 1913), 370–424.

Kaplan, Lawrence. "Jefferson, the Napoleonic Wars, and the Balance of Power." *William and Mary Quarterly*, 3d ser., XIV (April, 1957), 193–217.

Lauterpacht, Hersch. "The Grotian Tradition in International Law." *British Yearbook of International Law*, XXIII (1946), 1–53.

Lint, Gregg. "The American Revolution and the Law of Nations, 1776–1789." *Diplomatic History*, I (Winter, 1977), 20–34.

Peterson, Merrill. "Thomas Jefferson and Commercial Policy, 1783–1793." *William and Mary Quarterly*, 3d ser., XXII (October, 1965), 584–610.

Rosen, Stephen P. "Alexander Hamilton and the Domestic Uses of International Law." *Diplomatic History*, V (Summer, 1981), 183–202.

Turner, Frederick J. "The Origin of Genêt's Projected Attack on Louisiana and the Floridas." *American Historical Review*, III (July, 1897), 650–71.

Turner, Frederick J. "The Policy of France Toward the Mississippi Valley in the Period of Washington and Adams." *American Historical Review*, X (January, 1905), 249–79.

Vagts, Alfred. "The United States and the Balance of Power." *Journal of Politics*, III (November, 1941), 392–440.

Vagts, Alfred, and Detlev Vagts. "The Balance of Power in International Law: A History of an Idea." *American Journal of International Law*, LXXIII (October, 1979), 555–80.

Walters, Leroy. "The Just War and the Crusade: Antitheses or Analogies?" *Monist*, LVII (October, 1973), 584–94.

Wright, Quincy. "International Law and Ideologies." *American Journal of International Law*, XLVIII (October, 1954), 615–30.

Index

Index

France
—balance of power and: as threat to, 7,
37, 92, 101, 119–21, 124, 129, 130,
157–58; as protector of, 7, 128–29;
Hume on, 38–39; in North America,
72, 73*n*
—relations with Great Britain: rivalry
of, 7, 33, 41, 42, 44–45, 68, 105,
128, 142; at war, 15, 45, 47, 68–69,
71–72, 86–87, 89, 110, 119, 122,
143, 157–58
—relations with Spain: as allies, 68, 70,
72; and Louisiana, 77, 119, 121–22,
130–32, 142; effect of French Revolution on, 85–86, 132; peace restored, 109
—relations with the United States: as allies, 31–32, 69, 78, 105, 144; effect
of French Revolution on, 47, 85,
87–89, 93, 103–104, 119; commercial ties, 69, 77–78, 84–85; senti-
mental bonds, 78, 89, 104, 152–53;
the British and, 73, 90, 152; abroga-
tion of 1778 treaties, 119, 122–23;
quasi war, 119–24, 152–53. *See also*
Canada; Louisiana; West Indies
Freedom of the seas: undermines papal
authority, 5; championed by France,
33, 128; in American policy, 117,
144, 145, 152, 159. *See also* Neutrality, rights of
French Revolution: mass armies and, 9;
challenge to monarchy, 32, 33, 85,
101–103, 120, 141; and the United
States, 47, 85, 87–89, 91, 93, 103–
104, 107–108, 119, 141; as threat
to balance of power system, 85–87,
92, 101

Gentz, Friedrich von, 35, 35*n*, 57, 60
Great Britain
—balance of power and, 38, 41, 43,
128–29, 157–58, 160
—relations with France. *See* France, re-

lations with Great Britain
—relations with Spain: in Nootka
Sound crisis, 50, 85–86, 94–95,
130–31; as adversaries, 68, 70,
71–72, 109, 132; as allies, 86,
87, 132
—relations with the United States: war
of independence, 31, 58, 59*n*, 67–
70, 142, 145; neutral rights and, 33,
70, 89–90, 110–11, 117, 125–26,
129–30, 144–45, 154, 159–60;
American commerce, 71, 76–77, 90,
110, 124, 128, 147–49, 160; Treaty
of Paris, 73–75; Jay Treaty, 90, 110–
19, 132, 151–53; war of 1812,
pp. 148–49, 151, 159
Grotius, Hugo: on religious war, 4; on
natural law, 14, 29–30; and Vattel,
14, 15, 17, 18, 29–30, 31, 54, 61;
on prudence, 51; on neutral rights,
116–17; mentioned, 53, 55, 88,
95, 138
Gulick, Edward, 22, 45, 158

Hamilton, Alexander
—domestic policy: on manufacturers,
21, 124, 155; on commerce, 40,
115–16, 150–51; on public credit,
42, 84–85, 146, 153; on executive
power, 99–100, 106, 155
—foreign policy: on American weakness
in, 21, 95, 98, 103–104, 113, 118–
19, 124, 125, 146; on Nootka Sound
crisis, 50, 91, 92, 94–96, 160; Jay
Treaty, 74–75, 91, 111–18; and Mississippi, 81, 95, 123–24; cooperation
with Britain, 82–83, 95, 109, 119,
125–26, 127, 129–30, 160; on
American neutrality, 87–89, 93, 97,
99, 117–19, 123, 124–25, 129,
145, 159–60; on quasi war with
France, 91, 108–109, 113, 119–24,
125, 160; and war, 92–93, 107, 119,
124, 125; and commercial discrimina-

172

the League of Armed Neutrality, 70,
145; definition of, 117–18, 144–45,
125–26, 159–60. *See also* United
States, foreign policy of
Neutrality proclamation. *See* Proclamation of Neutrality

Paterson, William, 43–44, 45
Plato, 5
Poland: division of, 22, 44–45, 53, 60,
153; saves Europe from the Turks,
28; mentioned, 55. *See also* Napoleon
Proclamation of Neutrality, 1, 83, 87–
89, 94, 100, 105–106, 152. *See also*
United States, foreign policy of
Pufendorf, Samuel, 14, 51, 88, 95, 97,
138

Religious war, 3, 4, 24, 54, 59, 61, 102.
See also Crusade
Republic: internal threats to, 39, 42,
127, 130, 133–37, 141, 153, 155;
promotes arts, sciences, and com-
merce, 40; foreign policy of, 50, 106,
108–109, 118, 135, 137, 139–40
Rome, 6, 9, 37–39, 44, 49, 150
Rousseau, 45, 134, 141
Rufus. *See* King, Rufus

Spain: and South American Indians, 26,
27, 53; in Nootka Sound crisis, 50,
85–86, 130–31; and the United
States, 70–74, 78–79, 84, 95, 122–
24, 131–32, 143, 148. *See* France, relations with Spain; Great Britain, relations with Spain

Tyranny, 19, 29, 32, 52, 54, 104, 107,
109

United States, Constitution of, 39, 44,
68, 80–82, 100, 133, 146
United States, foreign policy of
—neutrality: moral superiority of, 26,

104–105, 118, 160–61; difficulty of
maintaining, 89–90, 98, 110–11,
145; desirability of, 69, 87–92 *passim*, 97–99, 104, 105, 108, 118–19,
125–26, 128–29, 145, 151–52, 154
—relations with France. *See* France, relations with the United States
—relations with Great Britain. *See* Great
Britain, relations with the United
States
—relations with Spain. *See* Spain
Universal empire. *See* Universal
monarchy
Universal monarchy, 5–9, 37–39, 59,
102, 124

Vattel, Emmerich de: life of, 9, 15;
works of, 9–10, 15–16; and Hobbes,
10, 14, 16, 19, 22, 25, 53; impact of,
11–12, 14, 65, 157; and Christian
Wolff, 16, 17. *See* Grotius, Hugo
—law of nations, principles of: supported by balance of power, 10, 17–
18, 21, 24, 35, 158–59, 162; treaty
obligations, 11, 34–36, 51, 56, 65,
88, 97, 138–39; right of free passage, 11, 26, 34, 54, 66, 95, 130; just
conduct in war, 11, 62–66, 114,
116; rights of neutrals, 11, 116–17;
basis of, 14, 16–18, 22–25; just
cause of war, 17–18, 25, 47–57,
124; nonintervention, 19–21, 24–
25, 29–30, 53, 102; voluntary law of
nations, 26, 30, 53, 59–61, 65
Vitoria, 4, 14, 30, 53–55 *passim*, 61

Walzer, Michael, 29, 42, 49, 101
Washington, George: first presidential
term, 82–86; proclamation of neutrality, 1, 45, 47, 87, 99, 106; Farewell Address, 32, 110, 118; mentioned, 78, 122
West Indies, 68–69, 71, 76–77, 88,
109, 140, 148–49